TEACH YOUR

COMPUTERS
& THE INTERNET

VISUALLY

IDG's **3-D Visual** Series

IDG BOOKS *From* **maranGraphics**

IDG Books Worldwide, Inc.
An International Data Group Company
Foster City, CA • Indianapolis • Chicago • Dallas

Teach Yourself Computers & the Internet Visually

Published by
IDG Books Worldwide, Inc.
An International Data Group Company
919 E. Hillsdale Blvd., Suite 400
Foster City, CA 94404
(415) 655-3000

Library of Congress Catalog Card No.:

ISBN: 0-7645-6002-6

Printed in the United States of America

10 9 8 7 6 5 4 3

Distributed in the United States by IDG Books Worldwide, Inc.

Distributed by Computer and Technical Books in Miami, Florida, for South America and the Caribbean; by Longman Singapore in Singapore, Malaysia, Thailand, and Korea; by Toppan Co. Ltd. in Japan; by IDG Communications HK in Hong Kong; by WoodsLane Pty. Ltd. in Australia and New Zealand; and by Transworld Publishers Ltd. in the U.K. and Europe.

For general information on IDG Books in the U.S., including information on discounts and premiums, contact IDG Books at 800-762-2974 or 317-895-5200.

For U.S. Corporate Sales and quantity discounts, contact maranGraphics at 800-469-6616.

For information on international sales of IDG Books, contact Helen Saraceni at 415-655-3021, Fax number 415-655-3295.

For information on translations, contact Marc Jeffrey Mikulich, Director of Rights and Licensing, at IDG Books Worldwide. Fax Number 415-655-3295.

For sales inquiries and special prices for bulk quantities, write to the address above or call IDG Books Worldwide at 415-655-3000.

For information on using IDG Books in the classroom, or ordering examination copies, contact Jim Kelly at 800-434-2086.

Trademark Acknowledgments

**© 1995, 1996
maranGraphics, Inc.**

The 3-D illustrations are the
copyright of maranGraphics, Inc.

U.S. Corporate Sales	**U.S. Trade Sales**
Contact maranGraphics at (800) 469-6616 or Fax (905) 890-9434.	Contact IDG Books at (800) 434-3422 or (415) 655-3000.

Welcome to the world of IDG Books Worldwide.

IDG Books Worldwide, Inc., is a subsidiary of International Data Group, the world's largest publisher of computer-related information and the leading global provider of information services on information technology. IDG was founded more than 25 years ago and now employs more than 8,500 people worldwide. IDG publishes more than 270 computer publications in over 75 countries (see listing below). More than 90 million people read one or more IDG publications each month.

Launched in 1990, IDG Books Worldwide is today the #1 publisher of best-selling computer books in the United States. We are proud to have received eight awards from the Computer Press Association in recognition of editorial excellence and three from Computer Currents' First Annual Readers' Choice Awards. Our best-selling ...For Dummies® series has more than 25 million copies in print with translations in 30 languages. IDG Books Worldwide, through a joint venture with IDG's Hi-Tech Beijing, became the first U.S. publisher to publish a computer book in the People's Republic of China. In record time, IDG Books Worldwide has become the first choice for millions of readers around the world who want to learn how to better manage their businesses.

Our mission is simple: Every one of our books is designed to bring extra value and skill-building instructions to the reader. Our books are written by experts who understand and care about our readers. The knowledge base of our editorial staff comes from years of experience in publishing, education, and journalism - experience which we use to produce books for the '90s. In short, we care about books, so we attract the best people. We devote special attention to details such as audience, interior design, use of icons, and illustrations. And because we use an efficient process of authoring, editing, and desktop publishing our books electronically, we can spend more time ensuring superior content and spend less time on the technicalities of making books.

You can count on our commitment to deliver high-quality books at competitive prices on topics you want to read about. At IDG Books Worldwide, we continue in the IDG tradition of delivering quality for more than 25 years. You'll find no better book on a subject than one from IDG Books Worldwide.

John Kilcullen
President and CEO
IDG Books Worldwide, Inc.

IDG Books Worldwide, Inc., is a subsidiary of International Data Group, the world's largest publisher of computer-related information and the leading global provider of information services on information technology. International Data Group publishes over 276 computer publications in over 75 countries. Ninety million people read one or more International Data Group publications each month. International Data Group's publications include: Argentina: Annuario de Informatica, Computerworld Argentina, PC World Argentina; Australia: Australian Macworld, Client/Server Journal, Computer Living, Computerworld, Computerworld 100, Digital News, IT Casebook, Network World, On-line World Australia, PC World, Publishing Essentials, Reseller, WebMaster; Austria: Computerwelt Osterreich, Networks Austria, PC Tip; Belarus: PC World Belarus; Belgium: Data News; Brazil: Annuário de Informática, Computerworld Brazil, Connections, Super Game Power, Macworld, PC Player, PC World Brazil, Publish Brazil, Reseller News; Bulgaria: Computerworld Bulgaria, Networkworld/Bulgaria, PC & MacWorld Bulgaria; Canada: CIO Canada, Client/Server World, Computerworld Canada, InfoCanada, Network World Canada; Chile: Computerworld Chile, PC World Chile; Colombia: Computerworld Colombia, PC World Colombia; Costa Rica: PC World Centro America; The Czech and Slovak Republics: Computerworld Czechoslovakia, Elektronika Czechoslovakia, Macworld Czech Republic, PC World Czechoslovakia, Denmark. Communications World, Computerworld Danmark, Macworld Danmark, PC Privat Danmark, PC World Danmark, PC World Danmark Supplements, TECH World; Dominican Republic: PC World Republica Dominicana; Ecuador: PC World Ecuador; Egypt: Computerworld Middle East, PC World Middle East; El Salvador: PC World Centro America; Finland: MikroPC, Tietoverkko, Tietoviikko; France: Distributique, Golden, Hebdo-Distributique, Info PC, Le Guide du Monde Informatique, Le Monde Informatique, Reseaux & Telecoms; Germany: Computer Partner, Computerwoche, Computerwoche Extra, Computerwoche Focus, I/M Information Management, Macwelt, PC Welt; Greece: GamePro, Multimedia World; Guatemala: PC World Centro America; Honduras: PC World Centro America; Hong Kong: Computerworld Hong Kong, PCWorld Hong Kong, Publish in Asia; Hungary: ABCD CD-ROM, Computerworld Szamitastechnika, PC & Mac World Hungary, PC-X Magazine; Iceland: Tolvuheimur/PC World Island; India: Information Systems Computerworld, PC World India, Publish in Asia; Indonesia: InfoKomputer PC World, Komputek Computerworld, Publish in Asia; Ireland: ComputerScope, PC Live!; Israel: People & Computers; Italy: Computerworld Italia, Computerworld Italia Special Editions, Macworld Italia, Networking Italia, PC Shopping, PC World Italia, PC World/Walt Disney; Japan: DTP World, HP Open World Japan, Macworld Japan, Nikkei Personal Computing, Open World Japan, OS/2 World Japan, SunWorld Japan, Windows World Japan; Kenya: East African Computer News; Korea: Hi-Tech Information/Computerworld, Macworld Korea, PC World Korea; Macedonia: PC World Macedonia; Malaysia: Computerworld Malaysia, PC World Malaysia, Publish in Asia; Mexico: Computerworld Mexico, Macworld, PC World Mexico; Myanmar: PC World Myanmar; Netherlands: Computer! Totaal, LAN Magazine, LanWorld Buyers Guide, Macworld, Net Magazine, Totaal! Beurskrant; New Zealand: Absolute Beginner's Guide, Computer Buyer, Computer Industry Directory, Computerworld New Zealand, MTB, Network World, PC World New Zealand; Nicaragua: PC World Centro America; Nigeria: PC World Nigeria; Norway: Computerworld Norge, Computerworld Privat (Datamagasinet), CW Rapport Norge, IDG's KURSGUIDE, Macworld Norge, Multimediaworld, PC World Ekspress, PC World Nettverk, PC World Norge, PC World's Produktguide, Windows World Spesial; Pakistan: Computerworld Pakistan, PC World Pakistan; Panama: PC World Panama; P. R. of China: China Computer Users, China Computerworld, China Infoworld, China Telecom World Weekly, Computer & Communication, Electronic Design China, Electronics Today, Electronics Weekly, Game Camp, Game Soft, Network World China, PC World China, Popular Computer Weekly, Software Weekly, Software World, Telecom World; Peru: Computerworld Peru, PC World Profesional Peru, PC World Peru; Poland: Computerworld Poland, Computerworld Special Report, Macworld, Networld, PC World Komputer; Philippines: Computerworld Philippines, PC World Philippines, Publish in Asia; Portugal: Cerebro/PC World, Computerworld/Correio Informático, Dealer World Portugal, Mac*In/PC*In, Multimedia World Portugal; Puerto Rico: PC World Puerto Rico; Romania: Computerworld Romania, PC World Romania, Telecom Romania; Russia: Computerworld Russia, Mir PK, Sety; Singapore: Computerworld Singapore, PC World Singapore, Publish in Asia; Slovenia: MONITOR; South Africa: Computing S.A., InfoWorld S.A., Network World S.A., Software World; Spain: Computerworld Espa-a, COMUNICACIONES WORLD, Dealer World, Macworld Espa-a, PC World Espa-a; Sweden: CAP&Design, Computer Sweden, Corporate Computing, MacWorld, Maxi Data, MikroDatorn, Natverk & Kommunikation, PC/Aktiv, PC World, Windows World; Switzerland: Computerworld Schweiz, Macworld Schweiz, PCtip; Taiwan: Computerworld Taiwan, Macworld Taiwan, PC World Taiwan, Publish Taiwan, Windows World; Thailand: Thai Computerworld, Publish in Asia; Turkey: Computerworld Turkiye, MACWORLD Turkiye, PC WORLD Turkiye; Ukraine: Computerworld Kiev, Computers & Software, Multimedia World Ukraine, PC World Ukraine; United Kingdom: Acorn User, Amiga Action, Amiga Computing, Appletalk, Computing, GamePro, Macworld, Network News, Parents and Computers, PC Advisor, PC Home, PSX Pro UK, The WEB; United States: Cable in the Classroom, CD Review, CIO Magazine, Computerworld, Computerworld Client/Server Journal, Digital Video Magazine, DOS World, Federal Computer Week, GamePro, InfoWorld, I-Way, JavaWorld, Macworld, Multimedia World, Netscape World Online, Network World, PC Entertainment, PC World, Publish, SunWorld Online, SWATPro Magazine, Video Event, WebMaster; Uruguay: PC World Uruguay; Venezuela: Computerworld Venezuela, PC World Venezuela; and Vietnam: PC World Vietnam.

**Every maranGraphics book represents
the extraordinary vision and commitment of a unique family:
the Maran family of Toronto, Canada.**

Back Row (from left to right): *Sherry Maran, Rob Maran, Richard Maran,
Maxine Maran, Jill Maran.*

Front Row (from left to right): *Judy Maran, Ruth Maran.*

Richard Maran is the company founder and its inspirational leader. He developed maranGraphics' proprietary communication technology called "visual grammar." This book is built on that technology—empowering readers with the easiest and quickest way to learn about computers.

Ruth Maran is the Author and Architect—a role Richard established that now bears Ruth's distinctive touch. She creates the words and visual structure that are the basis for the books.

Judy Maran is the Project Manager. She works with Ruth, Richard, and the highly talented maranGraphics illustrators, designers, and editors to transform Ruth's material into its final form.

Rob Maran is the Technical and Production Specialist. He makes sure the state-of-the-art technology used to create these books always performs as it should.

Sherry Maran manages the Reception, Order Desk, and any number of areas that require immediate attention and a helping hand.

Jill Maran is a jack-of-all-trades and dynamo who fills in anywhere she's needed anytime she's back from university.

Maxine Maran is the Business Manager and family sage. She maintains order in the business and family—and keeps everything running smoothly.

CREDITS

Author & Architect:
Ruth Maran

Copy Developers & Editors:
Kelleigh Wing
Alison MacAlpine

Technical Reviewers:
Maarten Heilbron
Paul Whitehead

Project Manager:
Judy Maran

Editors:
Karen Derrah
Diana MacPherson

Layout & Cover Design:
Christie Van Duin

Illustrators:
Tamara Poliquin
Chris K.C. Leung
Russell Marini
Andrew Trowbridge
Julie Lane

Indexer:
Kelleigh Wing

Screen Shot Permissions:
Jill Maran

Post Production:
Robert Maran

ACKNOWLEDGMENTS

Thanks to the dedicated staff of maranGraphics, including
Susan Beytas, Noel Clannon, Karen Derrah, Francisco Ferreira,
Brad Hilderley, Julie Lane, Chris K.C. Leung, Alison MacAlpine,
Jill Maran, Judy Maran, Maxine Maran, Robert Maran, Sherry Maran,
Russ Marini, Tamara Poliquin, Andrew Trowbridge, Christie Van Duin,
Paul Whitehead and Kelleigh Wing.

Finally, to Richard Maran who originated the easy-to-use graphic
format of this guide. Thank you for your inspiration and guidance.

Screen Shot Permissions

All About Kids screen shot used with permission.

AltaVista screen shot reprinted with permission. AltaVista and the AltaVista logo are trademarks and service marks of Digital Equipment Corporation.

AMD chip used with permission from Advanced Micro Devices Inc. Copyright © 1995 Advanced Micro Devices, Inc. Reprinted with permission of copyright owner. All other rights reserved. AMD, the AMD logo, AMD 5x86, and 5x86 are trademarks of Advanced Micro Devices, Inc. and may not be used in advertising or publicity pertaining to distribution of this information without specific, written prior permission.

America Online screen reprinted with permission. Copyright 1996 America Online, Inc. All Rights Reserved.

American Stock Exchange screen shot used with permission.

Apple, the Apple Logo and Macintosh are registered trade marks of Apple Computer, Inc. Used with permission.

ArchiePlexForm used with permission from Nexor.

Complete Works of Shakespeare screen shot used with permission from Jeremy Hylton.

CompuServe screen shot reprinted with permission. CompuServe is a registered trademark of CompuServe Incorporated.

Copy Graphics screen shot used with permission from Terranet. Screen shot used on page 210. Terranet www.terranet.ab.ca Phone (403) 539-6972 Fax (403) 539-6993

CyberDance screen shot used with permission.

Cyrix chip used with permission. Cyrix Corporation, (http://www.cyrix.com), headquartered in Richardson, Texas, is a leading supplier of high-performance processors and systems to the personal computer industry. Founded in 1988, the company designs, manufactures and markets innovative x86 software-compatible processors for the desktop and mobile computer markets. The Cyrix 6x86 processor was recently recognized for its performance with awards from a number of publications, including Byte Magazine's Best Technology at CeBIT '96, PC Week's Corporate IT Excellence Award and Windows Sources' Stellar Award.

Dell computer logo used with permission from Dell Corporation.

Empire Mall screen shot reprinted with permission.

Energy Star logo reprinted with permission from Environmental Protection Agency (EPA).

Eudora screen reprinted with permission from Qualcomm.

FlowerStop screen reprinted with permission.

Global Chat screen used with permission from Quarterdeck.

golf.com screen shot used with permission.

Grammar Rock screen shot used with permission from Creative Wonders. Screen shot used on page 100.

Infoseek screen shot reprinted by permission. Infoseek, Infoseek Guide, Infoseek Personal and the Infoseek logo are trademarks of Infoseek Corporation which may be registered in certain jurisdictions. Copyright © 1995, 1996 Infoseek Corporation. All rights reserved.

Intel chips used with permission. Intel386™ and Intel486™ are trademarks of Intel Corporation. Pentium, Pentium Pro and OverDrive are registered trademarks of Intel Corporation in the U.S. and other countries.

Internet Phone screen shots reprinted with permission from VocalTec.

Iomega Zip drive used with permission from Iomega.

Le Grand Louvre screen shot reprinted with permission.

Library of Congress screen (from their FTP site) used with permission from the Library of Congress.

Lycos screen shot reprinted with permission. Copyright © 1996 Lycos, Inc. All Rights Reserved. The Lycos™ "Catalog of the Internet" Copyright © 1994-1995, 1996 Carnegie Mellon University. All Rights Reserved. Used by permission. Screen shots to be included: Two "screen shots" of the Lycos home page URL http://www.lycos.com

Marx Brothers screen shot used with permission.

Mavis Beacon Teaches Typing reprinted with permission from Mindscape.

Microsoft box shot of Microsoft Office Packaged Product reprinted with permission from Microsoft Corporation.

Microsoft screen shots of Microsoft Golf, Microsoft Musical Instruments and Microsoft Dinosaurs reprinted with permission from Microsoft Corporation. Images from Dorling Kindersley.

Microsoft screen shots of Windows 95, Windows 3.1, Access 95, Access for Windows 3.1, Excel 95, Excel 5, Word 95, Word 6, DOS 6.2, PowerPoint 95, PowerPoint for Windows 3.1, MSN and Internet Explorer reprinted by permission of Microsoft Corporation.

National Library of Medicine screen shot used with permission.

Netscape screens used with permission. Netscape and Netscape Navigator are trademarks of Netscape Communications Corp.

Online Vacation Mall screen shot used with permission Copyright 1996, Mark Net World.

Shareware.com screen shot reprinted with permission from CNET: The Computer Network, copyright 1996.

SkiSoft screen shot reprinted with permission. Copyright © 1995, 1996 by SkiSoft, Inc. All rights reserved.

Star Chefs screen shot used with permission. Copyright 1996 Boiling Water, Inc. All rights reserved.

Submit It! screen shot reprinted with permission. Copyright 1995-1996 Submit It! Inc. All Rights Reserved.

USA TODAY screen shot used with permission.

WebChat screen used with permission from WebChat.

Worlds Inc. screen shots used with permission. Screen shots used on page 266.

Yahoo screen shot reprinted with permission. Text and artwork copyright © 1996 by YAHOO!, Inc. All rights reserved. YAHOO! and the YAHOO! logo are trademarks of YAHOO!, Inc.

TABLE OF CONTENTS

TABLE OF CONTENTS

CHAPTER 1 *Introduction to Computers*

CHAPTER 2 *Input and Output*

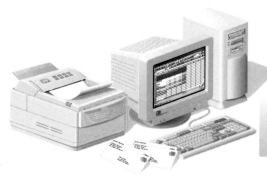

CHAPTER 3 *Processing*

CHAPTER 4 *Storage Devices*

CHAPTER 5 *Portable Computers*

TABLE OF CONTENTS

CHAPTER 9 *The Internet*

CHAPTER 10 *The World Wide Web*

TABLE OF CONTENTS

CHAPTER 13 *Mailing Lists*

CHAPTER 14 *Newsgroups and Chat*

CHAPTER 15 *FTP*

Need help using your new computer? This chapter will help you get started.

CHAPTER 1

INTRODUCTION TO COMPUTERS

HARDWARE AND SOFTWARE

Hardware and software are the two basic parts of a computer system.

HARDWARE

Hardware is any part of a computer system you can see or touch.

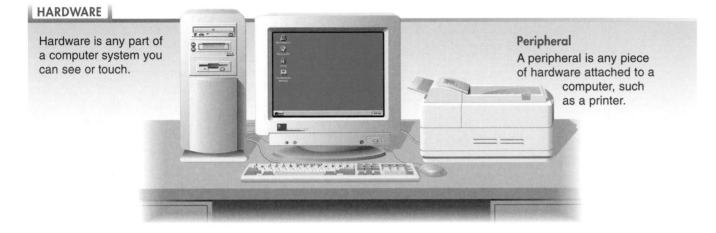

Peripheral

A peripheral is any piece of hardware attached to a computer, such as a printer.

SOFTWARE

Software is a set of electronic instructions that tell a computer what to do. You cannot see or touch software, but you can see and touch the packaging the software comes in.

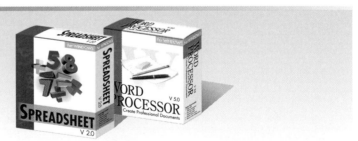

Application Software

Application software lets you accomplish specific tasks. Popular application software includes Microsoft® Word and Lotus 1-2-3.

Operating System Software

Operating system software controls the overall activity of a computer. Most new computers come with the Windows 95 operating system software.

GETTING HELP

When using new hardware and software, there are many places where you can get help.

Documentation

Hardware and software should come with printed documentation that tells you how to set up and use the product. Many software packages also come with a built-in help feature. You can also check local book stores for manuals with detailed, step-by-step instructions.

Call the Experts

If you have questions about setting up or using new hardware or software, try calling the store where you purchased the product.

Classes

Colleges and computer stores often offer computer courses. Many communities also have computer clubs where you can ask questions and exchange ideas.

HOW COMPUTERS WORK

A computer collects, processes, stores and outputs information.

INPUT

You use input devices to communicate with a computer. Input devices let you enter information and issue commands. A keyboard, mouse and joystick are input devices.

PROCESS

The Central Processing Unit (CPU) is the main chip in a computer. The CPU processes instructions, performs calculations and manages the flow of information through a computer system. The CPU communicates with input, output and storage devices to perform tasks.

STORE

A storage device holds information. The computer uses information stored on these devices to perform tasks. A hard drive and a floppy disk are storage devices.

OUTPUT

An output device lets a computer communicate with you. These devices display information on a screen, create printed copies or generate sound. A monitor, printer and speakers are output devices.

BYTES

Bytes are used to measure the amount of information a device can store.

Byte

One byte is one character. A character can be a number, letter or symbol.

One byte consists of eight bits (binary digits). A bit is the smallest unit of information a computer can process.

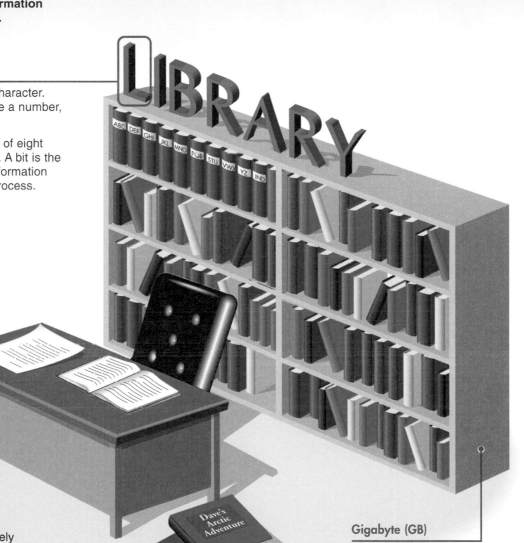

Kilobyte (K)

One kilobyte is 1,024 characters. This is approximately equal to one page of double-spaced text.

Megabyte (MB)

One megabyte is 1,048,576 characters. This is approximately equal to one novel.

Gigabyte (GB)

One gigabyte is 1,073,741,824 characters. This is approximately equal to one thousand novels.

TYPES OF COMPUTER SYSTEMS

**There are several types
of computer systems.**

PC (PERSONAL COMPUTER)

A PC is a computer
designed to meet the
needs of one person
and usually refers
to IBM-compatible
computers. PCs
are found in many
businesses and are
popular for home use.

MACINTOSH

Macintosh computers are
found in many homes
and are very popular in
the graphics, publishing
and multimedia industries.
The Macintosh was the
first widely-used computer
that offered a graphical
display.

MAINFRAME

A mainframe is a computer that
can process and store large
amounts of information and
support many users at the
same time. Mainframes
are often used by
banks and insurance
companies.

Mainframes process and store
information entered on terminals.
A terminal consists of a keyboard
and monitor and is simply used to
input and output
information.

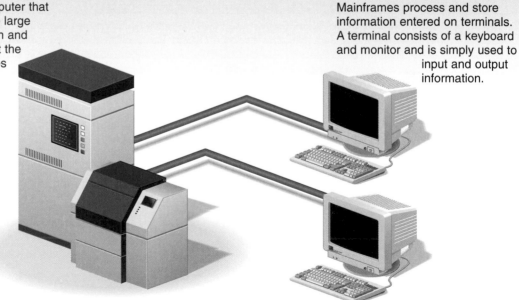

A TYPICAL COMPUTER

A typical computer system consists of several parts.

Computer Case
A computer case contains all the major components of a computer system.

Monitor
A monitor is a device that displays text and images generated by the computer.

Printer
A printer is a device that produces a paper copy of documents you create on the computer.

Modem
A modem is a device that lets computers communicate through telephone lines. A modem can also be found inside the computer case.

Keyboard
A keyboard is a device that lets you type information and instructions into a computer.

Mouse
A mouse is a hand-held device that lets you select and move items on the screen.

INSIDE A COMPUTER

All computers contain the same basic components.

Power Supply

A power supply changes normal household electricity into electricity that a computer can use.

Hard Drive

A hard drive is the primary device that a computer uses to store information.

Expansion Card

An expansion card lets you add new features to a computer. For example, an expansion card can give a computer the ability to record and play sound.

Expansion Slot

An expansion slot is a socket on the motherboard. An expansion card plugs into an expansion slot.

Motherboard

A motherboard is the main circuit board of a computer. All electrical components plug into the motherboard.

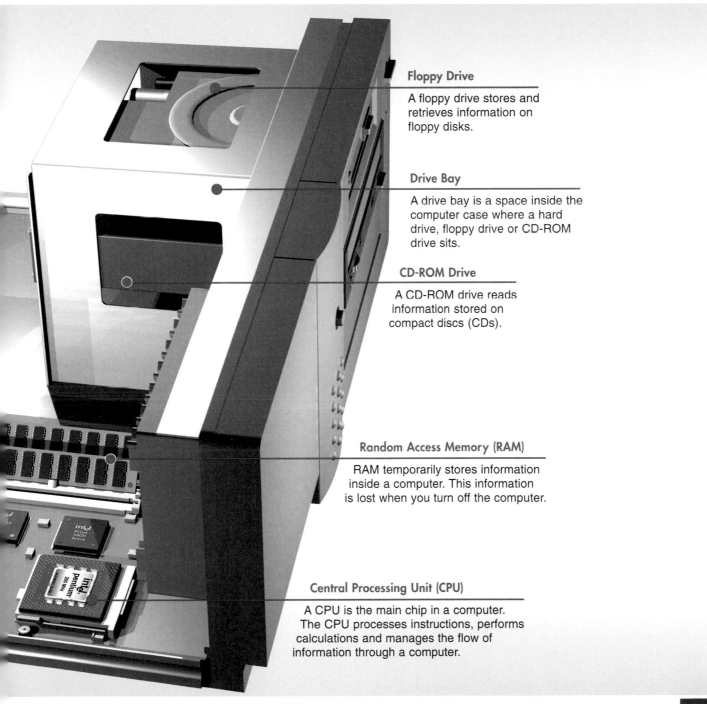

Floppy Drive

A floppy drive stores and retrieves information on floppy disks.

Drive Bay

A drive bay is a space inside the computer case where a hard drive, floppy drive or CD-ROM drive sits.

CD-ROM Drive

A CD-ROM drive reads information stored on compact discs (CDs).

Random Access Memory (RAM)

RAM temporarily stores information inside a computer. This information is lost when you turn off the computer.

Central Processing Unit (CPU)

A CPU is the main chip in a computer. The CPU processes instructions, performs calculations and manages the flow of information through a computer.

COMPUTER CASE

A computer case contains all the major components of a computer system.

The amount of space a computer case takes up on a desk or the floor is called the footprint. The footprint is usually measured in square inches.

DESKTOP CASE

A desktop case usually sits on a desk, under a monitor.

TOWER CASE

A tower case usually sits on the floor. This provides more desk space, but can be less convenient for inserting and removing floppy disks and CD-ROM discs.

ALL-IN-ONE CASE

An all-in-one case contains a monitor, disk drives, CD-ROM drive and speakers in a single unit.

PORTABLE

A portable is a small, lightweight computer that you can easily transport. A portable has a built-in keyboard and screen.

POWER SUPPLY

A power supply changes the alternating current (AC) that comes from an outlet to the direct current (DC) that a computer can use.

A fan inside the power supply prevents the elements inside a computer from overheating.

The capacity of a power supply is measured in watts. An average computer uses up to 200 watts, whereas an average light bulb uses 60 watts.

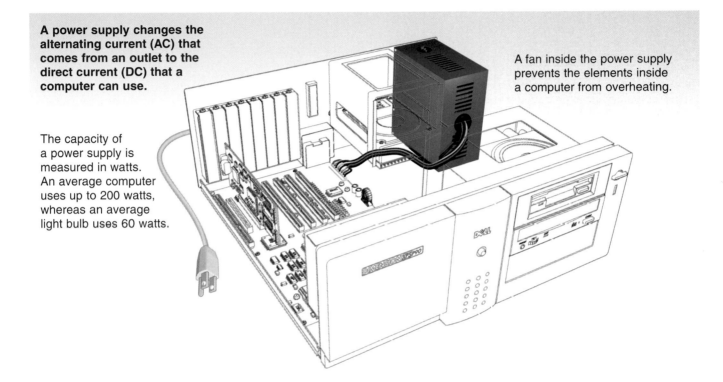

PROTECT YOUR EQUIPMENT

Changes in electrical power can damage equipment and information.

Surge Protector

A surge protector, or surge suppressor, guards a computer against surges. A surge is a fluctuation in power. These fluctuations happen most often during storms.

UPS

An Uninterruptible Power Supply (UPS) protects a computer from a loss of power. A UPS contains a battery that stores electrical power. If the power fails, the battery can run the computer for a short time so you can save your information.

PORT

A port is a connector at the back of a computer where you plug in an external device such as a printer or modem. This allows instructions and data to flow between the computer and the device.

Parallel Port

A parallel port has 25 holes. This type of port is known as a female connector. A parallel port connects a printer or tape drive.

There are two enhanced types of parallel ports—Enhanced Parallel Port (EPP) and Extended Capabilities Port (ECP). These types of parallel ports increase the speed at which information flows between the computer and a device.

A computer internally labels each parallel port with the letters LPT. The first parallel port is named LPT1, the second parallel port is named LPT2, and so on.

Monitor Port

A monitor port connects a monitor.

Serial Port

A serial port has either 9 or 25 pins. This type of port is known as a male connector. A serial port connects a mouse or modem.

A computer internally labels each serial port with the letters COM. The first serial port is named COM1, the second serial port is named COM2, and so on.

Keyboard Port

A keyboard port connects a keyboard.

Game Port

A game port connects a joystick.

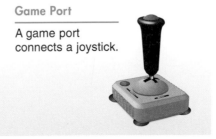

USB

Universal Serial Bus (USB) is a new type of port that provides a way to connect multiple devices using only one port. For example, you can connect a printer, modem, joystick and scanner to a single USB port.

EXPANSION CARD

An expansion card is a circuit board that lets you add a new feature to a computer.

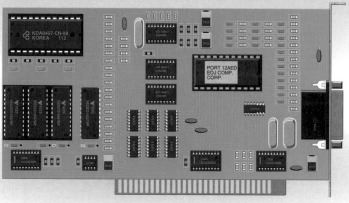

KDA0457-CN-09
KOREA   112

PORT 12AED
EDJ COMP.
CORP.

An expansion card is also called an expansion board.

EXPANSION SLOT

An expansion slot is a socket where you plug in an expansion card.

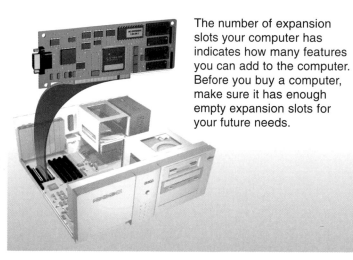

The number of expansion slots your computer has indicates how many features you can add to the computer. Before you buy a computer, make sure it has enough empty expansion slots for your future needs.

CONNECT DEVICES

Some expansion cards are accessible from the back of a computer. These expansion cards contain ports where you can plug in devices. For example, you can plug speakers into a sound card to hear the sound generated by the computer.

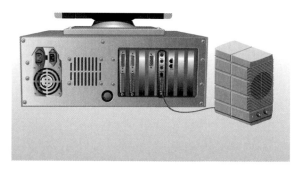

TYPES OF EXPANSION CARDS

A computer usually comes with one or more expansion cards.

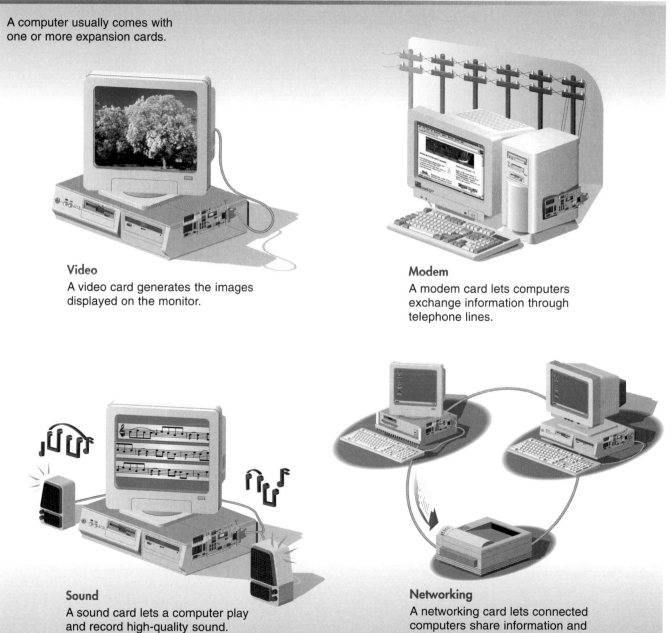

Video
A video card generates the images displayed on the monitor.

Modem
A modem card lets computers exchange information through telephone lines.

Sound
A sound card lets a computer play and record high-quality sound.

Networking
A networking card lets connected computers share information and equipment.

ERGONOMICS

PREVENT BACK STRAIN

You can avoid back strain by ensuring that your chair provides proper back support and by maintaining good posture at all times.

Ergonomics is the science of designing equipment for a safe and comfortable working environment.

Posture

Do not lean forward or slouch in your chair. You should shift positions often and stand up to stretch your arms and legs at least once an hour.

Chair

Look for a fully adjustable, comfortable chair that provides support for your lower back. Contoured chair seats help blood circulate more freely by relieving pressure on the legs.

Foot Rest

Make sure your feet are always flat on the floor. If your feet do not reach the floor, you can buy an adjustable foot rest or place your feet on a telephone book.

PREVENT WRIST STRAIN

You can avoid wrist strain when typing by keeping your elbows level with the keyboard and keeping your wrists straight and higher than your fingers.

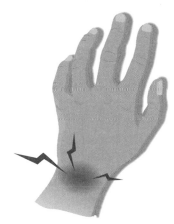

Carpal Tunnel Syndrome (CTS)

Carpal Tunnel Syndrome is a Repetitive Stress Injury (RSI) whose symptoms include numbness, tingling and pain in the fingers. The condition affects some workers who type without proper wrist support or type for long periods of time without breaks.

Wrist Rest

You can use a wrist rest with your keyboard to elevate your wrists and ensure they remain straight at all times. Some mouse pads also come with built-in wrist rests.

Keyboard Shelf

You can use a keyboard shelf to help keep your elbows level with the keyboard. A keyboard shelf lets you adjust the height and position of the keyboard and slides under the desk to provide more desk space. Many keyboard shelves come with a built-in mouse pad.

ERGONOMICS

PREVENT NECK STRAIN

You can avoid neck strain by placing the monitor where you can comfortably view the screen.

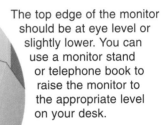

The top edge of the monitor should be at eye level or slightly lower. You can use a monitor stand or telephone book to raise the monitor to the appropriate level on your desk.

Monitor Arm
You can buy a fully-adjustable monitor arm to hold the monitor above the desktop. This lets you place the monitor in the best position for you. When you finish using the monitor, you can move the monitor out of the way.

Copyholder
You can use a copyholder to keep documents you are working on at eye level. This prevents you from constantly looking up and down from the screen to the desktop.

PREVENT EYE STRAIN

You can avoid eye strain by minimizing the amount of light that reflects off the computer screen.

You can also reduce eye strain by periodically exercising the muscles in your eyes. To do so, focus on a distant object, then focus on a close object. Repeat this several times. Perform the entire exercise a few times an hour.

Lighting

Overhead lights reflect light off the computer screen. A desk light or track light that is not pointed directly at the screen will help reduce eye strain.

Glare Filter

A glare filter fits over the front of a monitor to reduce the amount of glare from the screen. Glare filters can make text and images on the screen easier to read. Beware of glare filters that make the screen harder to view.

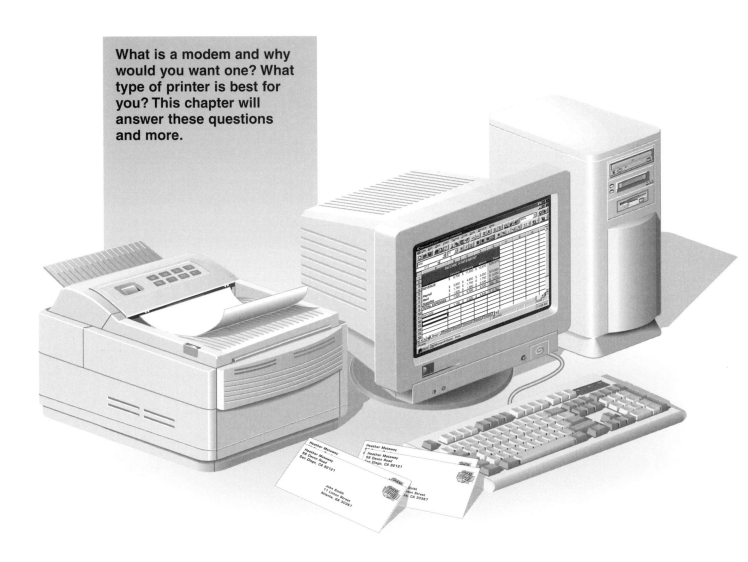

What is a modem and why would you want one? What type of printer is best for you? This chapter will answer these questions and more.

INPUT AND OUTPUT

MOUSE

A mouse is a hand-held device that lets you select and move items on your screen. A mouse can come in various shapes, colors and sizes.

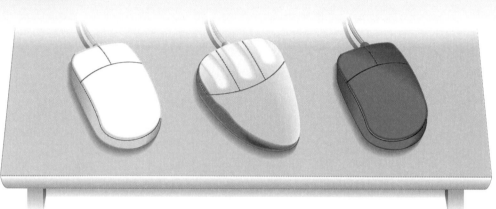

Most programs sold today are designed to work with a mouse. A mouse is essential when using Windows programs.

USE THE MOUSE

Resting your hand on the mouse, use your thumb and two rightmost fingers to move the mouse on the desk. Use your two remaining fingers to press the mouse buttons.

When you move the mouse on your desk, the pointer on the screen moves in the same direction. The pointer assumes different shapes (example: ⊳ or I) depending on its location on the screen and the task you are performing.

MOUSE ACTIONS

There are four mouse actions
you will commonly perform.

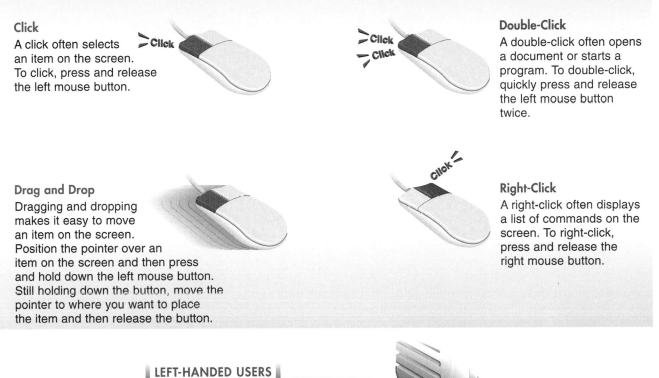

Click

A click often selects
an item on the screen.
To click, press and release
the left mouse button.

Double-Click

A double-click often opens
a document or starts a
program. To double-click,
quickly press and release
the left mouse button
twice.

Drag and Drop

Dragging and dropping
makes it easy to move
an item on the screen.
Position the pointer over an
item on the screen and then press
and hold down the left mouse button.
Still holding down the button, move the
pointer to where you want to place
the item and then release the button.

Right-Click

A right-click often displays
a list of commands on the
screen. To right-click,
press and release the
right mouse button.

LEFT-HANDED USERS

If you are left-handed, you can switch
the functions of the left and right
mouse buttons to make the mouse
easier to use. For example, to click
an item, you would press the right
button instead of the left.

MOUSE

MOUSE PAD

A mouse pad provides a smooth surface for moving the mouse and can brighten up your desktop. A mouse pad also reduces the amount of dirt that enters the mouse and protects your desk from scratches.

Hard plastic mouse pads tend to attract less dirt and provide a smoother surface than fabric mouse pads.

You can buy mouse pads displaying interesting designs or pictures at most computer stores. Some mouse pads have built-in wrist support for increased comfort.

CLEAN THE MOUSE

You should occasionally remove and clean the ball inside the mouse. Make sure you also remove dust and dirt from the inside to help ensure smooth motion of the mouse.

CORDLESS MOUSE

A cordless mouse runs on a battery and reduces the clutter on your desk by eliminating the mouse cord. When you move the mouse on your desk, the mouse sends signals through the air to your computer, the same way a remote control sends signals to a television.

OTHER POINTING DEVICES

Joystick

A joystick helps you control the movement of people and objects in many computer games. Joysticks are used for arcade-type computer games because they let you move quickly and accurately in any direction.

Touchpad

A touchpad is a surface that is sensitive to pressure and motion. When you move your fingertip across the pad, the pointer on the screen moves in the same direction.

Trackball

A trackball is an upside-down mouse that remains stationary on your desk. You roll the ball with your fingers or palm to move the pointer on the screen. A trackball is a great alternative to a mouse when you have limited desk space.

27

KEYBOARD

The keys on a keyboard let you enter information and instructions into a computer.

Most keyboards have 101 keys. Your keyboard may look different from the keyboard shown here.

Function Keys

These keys let you quickly perform specific tasks. For example, in many programs you can press **F1** to display help information.

Escape Key

You can press **Esc** to quit a task you are performing.

Caps Lock and Shift Keys

These keys let you enter text in upper (ABCD) and lower (abcd) case letters.

Press **Caps Lock** to change the case of all letters you type. Press the key again to return to the original case.

Press **Shift** in combination with another key to type an uppercase letter.

Ctrl and Alt Keys

You can use the **Ctrl** or **Alt** key in combination with another key to perform a specific task. For example, in some programs you can press **Ctrl** and **S** to save a document.

Spacebar

You can press the **Spacebar** to insert a blank space.

Backspace Key

You can press **Backspace** to remove the character to the left of the cursor.

Delete Key

You can press **Delete** to remove the character to the right of the cursor.

Status Lights

These lights indicate whether the **Num Lock** or **Caps Lock** features are on or off.

Numeric Keypad

When the **Num Lock** light is on, you can use the number keys (0 through 9) to enter numbers. When the **Num Lock** light is off, you can use these keys to move the cursor around the screen. To turn the light on or off, press **Num Lock**.

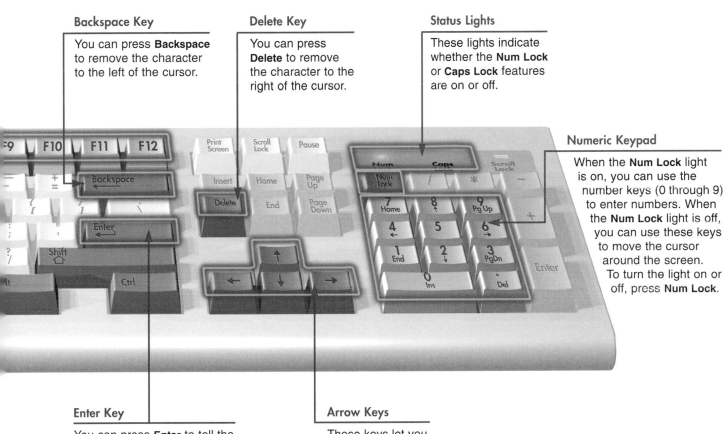

Enter Key

You can press **Enter** to tell the computer to carry out a task. In a word processing program, press this key to start a new paragraph.

Arrow Keys

These keys let you move the cursor around the screen.

KEYBOARD

Press Any Key

Many programs tell you to "press any key to continue." This simply means to press the **Spacebar**.

Typing Programs

There are programs available to help you improve your typing skills. You can buy these programs at most computer stores.

Special Characters

Many programs let you enter special characters or symbols that do not appear on the keyboard.

Position Your Hands

Most keyboards have small bumps on the **D** and **K** keys or on the **F** and **J** keys. These bumps help you position your fingers without looking at the keyboard.

Keyboard Shortcuts

Many programs let you select commands by using keyboard shortcuts. These shortcuts are often shown on the menus. For example, to select the **Save** command in some programs, you can press the **Ctrl** and **S** keys.

```
W Microsoft Word - letter
   File   Edit   View   Insert
   New...        Ctrl+N
   Open…         Ctrl+0
   Close
   Save          Ctrl+S
   Save As…
   Save All
```

A plus sign (+) between two key names tells you to press and hold down the first key before you press the second key.

Built-in Pointing Devices

You can buy keyboards with built-in pointing devices to select and move items on the screen. A built-in pointing device is a great alternative to a mouse when you have limited desk space.

Ergonomic Keyboards

Ergonomic keyboards position your hands naturally and support your wrists so you can work more comfortably. You can also buy a wrist rest for increased comfort.

PRINTER

A printer produces a paper copy of the information displayed on the screen.

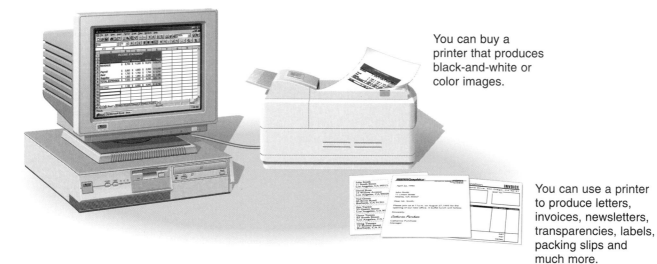

You can buy a printer that produces black-and-white or color images.

You can use a printer to produce letters, invoices, newsletters, transparencies, labels, packing slips and much more.

CHOOSE A PRINTER

There are several factors to consider when buying a printer.

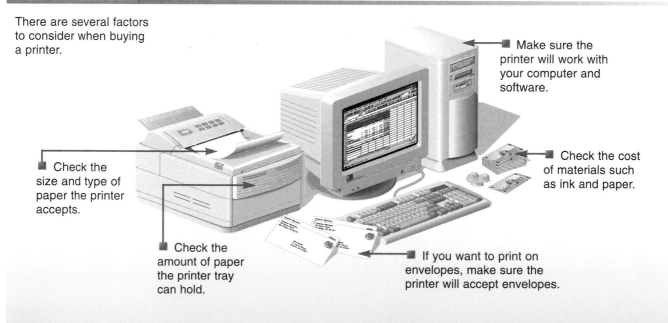

■ Make sure the printer will work with your computer and software.

■ Check the cost of materials such as ink and paper.

■ Check the size and type of paper the printer accepts.

■ Check the amount of paper the printer tray can hold.

■ If you want to print on envelopes, make sure the printer will accept envelopes.

PRINTER SPEED

The speed of a printer determines how quickly it can print the pages you selected. Speed is measured in characters per second (cps) or pages per minute (ppm). A higher speed results in faster output.

A complicated page, such as a page that contains graphics, takes longer to print than a page that contains only text.

PRINTER RESOLUTION

The resolution of a printer determines the quality of the images it can produce. A higher resolution results in sharper, more detailed images.

A printed image consists of thousands of tiny dots. A high resolution printer produces clearer images because the images are made up of a larger number of smaller dots.

300 dpi   600 dpi   1200 dpi

Printer resolution is measured in dots per inch (dpi). Generally, a resolution of 300 dpi is acceptable for most office documents, although 600 dpi printers are becoming the standard.

Resolution can also be expressed with two numbers (example: 600x300 dpi). These numbers describe the number of dots a printer can produce across and down in one square inch.

PRINTER

DOT-MATRIX PRINTER

A dot-matrix printer is the least expensive type of printer. This type of printer works by impact.

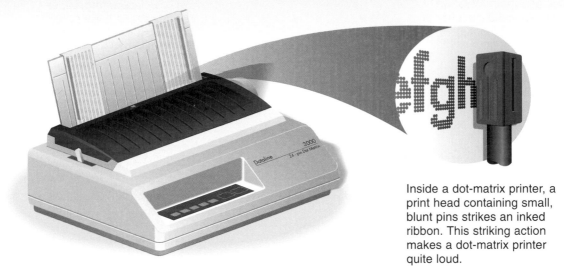

Inside a dot-matrix printer, a print head containing small, blunt pins strikes an inked ribbon. This striking action makes a dot-matrix printer quite loud.

Speed

Most dot-matrix printers produce images at a speed of 25 to 450 characters per second (cps) or 1 to 18 pages per minute (ppm).

Resolution

The resolution, or quality, of the images produced by a dot-matrix printer depends on the number of pins in the print head.

You can buy a 9-pin or 24-pin dot-matrix printer. A 9-pin dot-matrix printer produces draft-quality documents. A 24-pin printer produces typewriter-quality documents.

Ink

Dot-matrix printers store ink on ribbons similar to typewriter ribbons. When the ink runs out, you replace the ribbon.

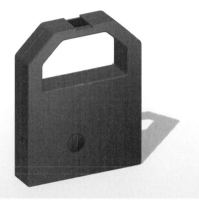

Paper

A dot-matrix printer typically uses continuous form paper. This paper has holes punched along each side and connects from end to end.

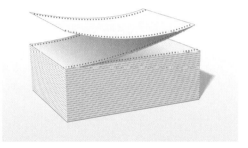

Narrow or Wide Carriage

You can buy either a narrow carriage or wide carriage dot-matrix printer. A narrow carriage printer accepts 8 1/2 by 11-inch paper. A wide carriage printer accepts many different paper sizes.

Multipart Forms

A dot-matrix printer is ideal for printing on multipart forms, which need an impact to print through multiple copies. Stores and courier companies frequently use multipart forms to print receipts.

PRINTER

INK JET PRINTER

An ink jet printer produces high-quality documents at a relatively low price. This type of printer is ideal for routine business and personal documents.

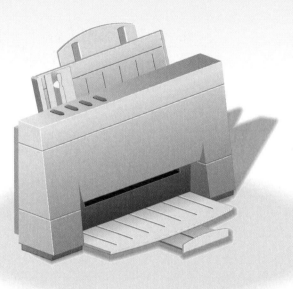

An ink jet printer has a print head that sprays ink through small holes onto a page.

Ink jet printers and Bubble Jet printers work the same way.

Speed
Most ink jet printers produce images at a speed of 0.5 to 4 pages per minute (ppm).

Resolution
The resolution, or quality, of the images produced by an ink jet printer ranges from 180 to 720 dots per inch (dpi).

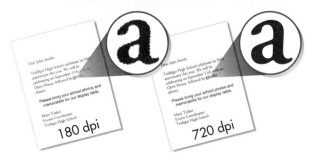

180 dpi

720 dpi

Ink

Ink jet printers use ink stored in cartridges. When the ink runs out, you replace the cartridge.

Look for smudge-resistant, fast-drying ink since images produced by an ink jet printer take time to dry and may smudge or smear if handled too soon.

Paper

Ink jet printers accept 8 1/2 by 11-inch paper. Some ink jet printers accept larger paper sizes.

Ink jet printers also accept envelopes, labels and transparencies. Specially-coated papers produce the best results when printing color images. Make sure you buy items designed specifically for use with ink jet printers.

Color

Color ink jet printers are very popular because they are less expensive than color laser printers and still produce high-quality color images.

A color ink jet printer sprays cyan, magenta, yellow and black ink to create images on a page. Lower-cost color ink jet printers create black by mixing the cyan, magenta and yellow ink. The best color images come from printers that offer black as a separate color.

PRINTER

LASER PRINTER

A laser printer is a high-speed printer that is ideal for business and personal documents and for proofing professional graphics work.

A laser printer works like a photocopier to produce high-quality images on a page.

Speed

Most laser printers produce images at a speed of 4 to 20 pages per minute (ppm).

Resolution

The resolution, or quality, of the images produced by a laser printer ranges from 300 to 1200 dots per inch (dpi).

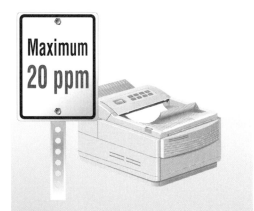

300 dpi

1200 dpi

Ink

Like photocopiers, laser printers use a fine powdered ink, called toner, which comes in a cartridge. When the toner runs out, you buy a new cartridge.

Paper

All laser printers can print on 8 1/2 by 11-inch paper, envelopes, labels and transparencies. Make sure you buy items designed specifically for use with laser printers.

Color

You can buy laser printers that produce color images. A color laser printer is more expensive than a color ink jet printer, but it produces superior output.

Multifunction

A multifunction laser printer can perform more than one task. This type of printer is often able to work as a fax machine, scanner and photocopier as well as a printer.

PRINTER

LASER PRINTER (CONTINUED)

Memory

Laser printers store pages in built-in memory before printing. A typical laser printer comes with 1 MB to 4 MB of memory.

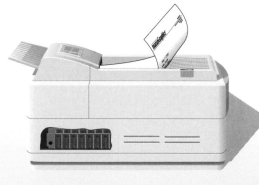

Memory is important for laser printers that produce images at high resolutions, such as 600 dpi. Memory is also important for laser printers that print on larger paper sizes and process complex print jobs.

You can often expand the amount of memory in a laser printer. Additional memory will increase the speed that the printer produces complex documents.

Laser Printer Languages

A printer language is software that tells a printer how to print a document. There are two types of laser printer languages—PCL and Postscript.

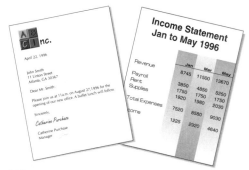

PCL

Most laser printers come with Printer Control Language (PCL). A PCL laser printer is less expensive, but does not offer the graphic capabilities and flexibility of a Postscript printer. The PCL language is popular for routine office tasks.

Postscript

A Postscript laser printer can handle more complex documents that include various colors, graphics and fonts. In addition, the same page will print exactly the same on any Postscript printer. The Postscript language is popular in the graphic arts industry, especially when the artwork will be sent to a professional print shop.

OTHER TYPES OF PRINTERS

There are three other types of printers that let you produce high-quality color images.

Solid Ink Printer

A solid ink printer produces high-quality color images at a relatively low price. This type of printer is ideal for producing crisp color images on regular paper and transparencies.

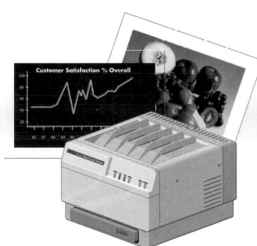

Thermal-Wax Printer

A thermal-wax printer produces sharp, rich, non-smearing images.

Dye Sublimation Printer

A dye sublimation printer is the most expensive type of printer and produces images that look like color photographs. Dye sublimation printers are also called thermal dye transfer printers.

PRINTER

PRINT FEATURES IN PROGRAMS

Computer programs offer many features to help you efficiently produce professional-looking documents.

Print Preview

Many programs have a print preview feature that lets you see on the computer screen what a page will look like when printed. This lets you perfect the layout of a page without having to print many drafts of the same document.

WYSIWYG

What You See Is What You Get (WYSIWYG, pronounced whiz-zee-wig) refers to a page that prints exactly as it appears on the computer screen.

This feature lets you see exactly what text and graphics will look like before you print a document. Most Windows programs are WYSIWYG.

Portrait and Landscape

Many programs let you print text or graphics in one of two directions on a page.

Portrait

Landscape

Portrait prints images across the short side of a page.

Landscape prints images across the long side of a page.

Envelopes and Labels

Many programs have a feature that lets you print on envelopes and labels.

Page Break

Programs often let you specify where you want one page to end and the next page to begin. When you have a document that covers many topics, you may want to put each topic on a different page.

Page Numbers

Many programs can automatically number the pages in a document. You can usually specify the position and style of the page numbers.

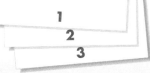

Print Manager

A print manager lets you keep track of documents you have sent to the printer. You can change the order of documents waiting to print and cancel the printing of a specific document. Windows comes with a built-in print manager.

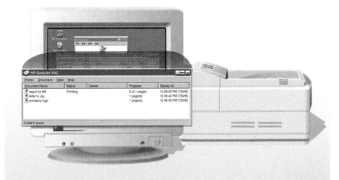

PRINTER

FONTS

Most printers come with a few built-in fonts, called resident fonts. Resident fonts print faster than the fonts stored on your computer.

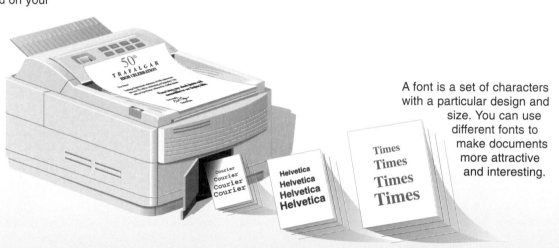

A font is a set of characters with a particular design and size. You can use different fonts to make documents more attractive and interesting.

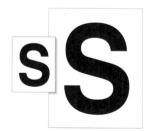

TrueType Font

A TrueType font generates characters using mathematical formulas. You can change the size of a TrueType font without distorting the font. A TrueType font will print exactly as it appears on the screen.

Bitmapped Font

A bitmapped font stores each character as a picture made up of a pattern of dots. If you change the size of a bitmapped font, the font may become distorted.

PRINT BUFFER AND SPOOLER

A computer can send data faster than a printer can accept and process the data. A print spooler or print buffer acts like a dam, holding the data and then releasing it at a speed the printer can handle.

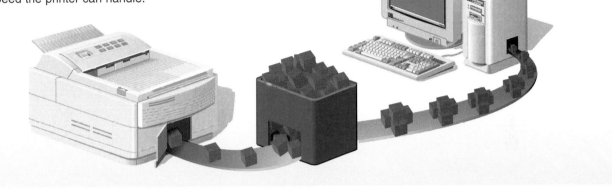

Print Buffer

A print buffer is a section of memory in a printer that stores information you selected to print. When the buffer is full, the computer must wait before sending more data to the printer.

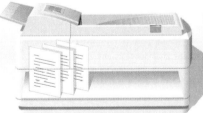

Print Spooler

A print spooler is a program on your computer that stores information you selected to print.

A print spooler can store more information than a print buffer and lets you continue using your computer without having to wait for a document to finish printing. Windows comes with a built-in print spooler.

MONITOR AND VIDEO CARD

The monitor and video card work together to display text and images on the screen.

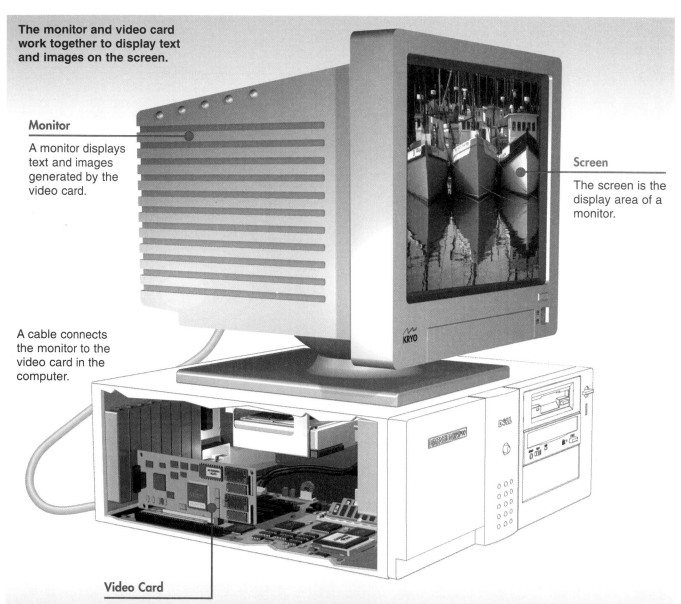

Monitor

A monitor displays text and images generated by the video card.

Screen

The screen is the display area of a monitor.

A cable connects the monitor to the video card in the computer.

Video Card

The video card is a circuit board that plugs into an expansion slot inside the computer. The video card translates instructions from the computer to a form the monitor can understand.

A video card is also called a video adapter, video board, graphics adapter, graphics board or graphics card.

CHOOSE A MONITOR

Size

The size of a monitor is measured diagonally across the screen. Common monitor sizes are 14, 15, 17 and 21 inches. Larger monitors are more expensive and ideal for desktop publishing, or working with graphics or large spreadsheets.

Manufacturers usually advertise the diagonal measurement of the picture tube inside the monitor, which is greater than the actual viewing area. Make sure you ask for the size of the viewing area.

Dot Pitch

The dot pitch is the distance between tiny dots on a screen. The dot pitch determines the sharpness of images on the screen. The smaller the dot pitch, the crisper the images. Select a monitor with a dot pitch of 0.28 mm or less.

Non-Interlaced

A non-interlaced monitor greatly reduces screen flicker. These monitors are more expensive than old, interlaced monitors, but reduce eye strain.

MONITOR AND VIDEO CARD

CHOOSE A MONITOR (CONTINUED)

Refresh Rate

The refresh rate determines the speed that a monitor redraws, or updates, images. The higher the refresh rate, the less flicker on the screen. This reduces eye strain.

The refresh rate is measured in hertz (Hz) and tells you the number of times per second the monitor redraws the entire screen. A monitor with a refresh rate of 72 Hz or more is recommended.

Controls

Monitors have controls to adjust the brightness, contrast and other features of the images displayed on the screen. You can find controls on the screen or on the monitor.

Tilt-and-Swivel Base

A tilt-and-swivel base lets you adjust the angle of the screen. This lets you reduce the glare from overhead lighting and view the screen more comfortably.

Electromagnetic Radiation

Any device that uses electricity produces electromagnetic radiation (EMR). You can protect yourself from potentially harmful effects by remaining a safe distance away from electrical devices.

Monitors emit EMR, but you can minimize the risk by buying a monitor that meets MPR II guidelines. The MPR II guidelines define acceptable levels of EMR.

You can further minimize the risk by turning off the monitor when it is not in use. Also avoid sitting near the sides or back of a monitor, which emit more EMR than the front.

The screen technology used in portable computers does not emit EMR.

ENERGY STAR

The Environmental Protection Agency (EPA) developed an energy-saving guideline called ENERGY STAR to reduce wasted energy and the pollution it causes.

When you do not use an ENERGY STAR computer for a period of time, the monitor enters an energy-saving sleep mode. You awaken the monitor by moving the mouse or pressing a key on the keyboard.

MONITOR AND VIDEO CARD

Screen Saver

A screen saver is a moving picture or pattern that appears on the screen when you do not use a computer for a period of time.

Screen savers were originally designed to prevent screen burn, which occurs when an image appears in a fixed position for a period of time.

Today's monitors are designed to prevent screen burn, but people still use screen savers for entertainment.

Windows provides several screen savers. You can purchase more sophisticated screen savers at most computer stores.

Glare Filter

A glare filter fits over the front of a monitor to reduce the amount of light reflected off the computer screen. This helps reduce eye strain.

Most glare filters also help block the radiation coming from the front of the monitor.

VIDEO CARD MEMORY

A video card has memory chips. These chips temporarily store information before sending it to the monitor.

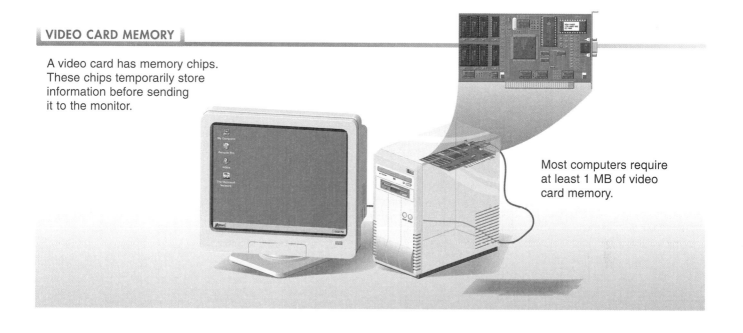

Most computers require at least 1 MB of video card memory.

DRAM

Dynamic Random Access Memory (DRAM) is the least expensive type of memory used on low to mid-range video cards. DRAM is adequate for routine office tasks.

VRAM

Video Random Access Memory (VRAM) is a form of DRAM specifically designed for video cards. VRAM is faster and more expensive than DRAM and is ideal for displaying colorful graphics.

DRAM and VRAM are the most common types of video card memory. Extended Data Out DRAM (EDO DRAM) and Window RAM (WRAM) are two other types of video card memory.

MONITOR AND VIDEO CARD

RESOLUTION

Resolution determines the amount of information a monitor can display.

Resolution is measured by the number of horizontal and vertical pixels. A pixel is the smallest element on the screen. Pixel is short for picture element.

A multisync monitor lets you adjust the resolution to suit your needs. Other monitors can only display one resolution.

| 640 x 480 | 800 x 600 | 1,024 x 768 | 1,280 x 1,024 |

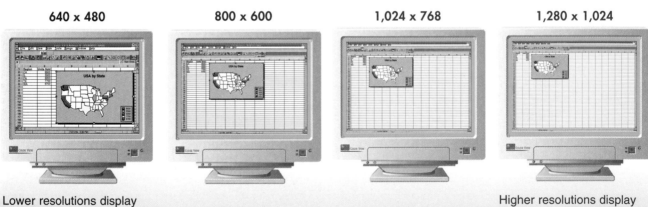

Lower resolutions display larger images so you can see information more clearly.

Higher resolutions display smaller images so you can display more information at once.

COLOR DEPTH

The number of colors a monitor can display determines how realistic images appear on a screen. More colors result in more realistic images.

VGA

Video Graphics Array (VGA) monitors display 16 colors at a resolution of 640 x 480. This is the minimum standard for computer systems.

SVGA

Super Video Graphics Array (SVGA) monitors display more colors and higher resolutions than VGA monitors. Most new computer systems offer SVGA.

16 Colors (4-bit color)	256 Colors (8-bit color)	65,536 Colors (16-bit color)	16,777,216 Colors (24-bit color)

Choppy-looking images.	Ideal for most home, business and game applications.	Ideal for video and desktop publishing applications. Unless you are a trained professional, it is difficult to distinguish between 16-bit and 24-bit color.	Ideal for photographic work. This setting is also called true color because it displays more colors than the human eye can distinguish.

MODEM

A modem lets computers exchange information through telephone lines.

A modem translates computer information into a form that can transmit over phone lines.

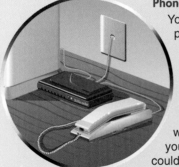

Phone Line

You do not need a separate phone line to use a modem. You can use the same phone line for telephone and modem calls. If your telephone and modem share the same line, make sure you turn off the call waiting feature when using your modem, since this feature could disrupt the modem connection.

The receiving modem translates the information it receives into a form the computer can understand.

MODEM APPLICATIONS

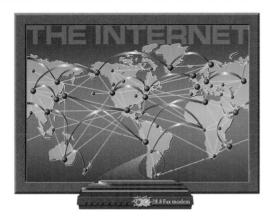

Connect to the Internet

A modem lets you connect to the Internet and online services such as America Online and CompuServe. This lets you access a vast amount of information and meet thousands of people with similar interests.

Exchange Information

When traveling or at home, you can use a modem to access information stored on the network at work. You can send and receive electronic messages (e-mail) and work with office files.

Send and Receive Faxes

Most modems can send and receive faxes. With a fax modem, you can create a document on your computer and then fax the document to another computer or fax machine.

When a computer receives a fax, the document appears on the screen. You can review and print the document, but you cannot edit the document unless you have Optical Character Recognition (OCR) software.

MODEM

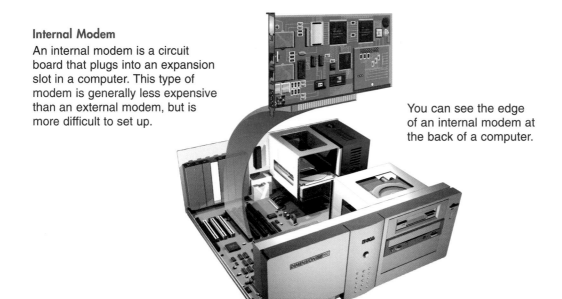

Internal Modem

An internal modem is a circuit board that plugs into an expansion slot in a computer. This type of modem is generally less expensive than an external modem, but is more difficult to set up.

You can see the edge of an internal modem at the back of a computer.

External Modem

An external modem is a small box that plugs into the back of a computer. An external modem takes up room on your desk, but you can use this type of modem with more than one computer.

Status lights on the modem tell you about the current transmission. For example, the RD light is on when the modem is receiving data.

If you are using an external modem with an older computer, make sure the computer uses a 16550 UART chip. This will ensure that the computer can handle current modem speeds. A UART chip controls the flow of information to and from the modem.

MODEM SPEED

The speed of a modem determines how fast it can send and receive information through telephone lines.

Modem speed is measured in bits per second (bps). You should buy a modem with a speed of at least 14,400 bps, but a 28,800 bps modem is recommended.

Modem speeds of 31,200 and 33,600 bps are now available.

Modem speed is also measured in kilobits per second (Kb/s). For example, a 28,800 bps modem is also referred to as a 28.8 Kb/s modem.

Save Time and Money

Buy the fastest modem you can afford. Faster modems transfer information more quickly. This will save you time and reduce online service charges and long distance charges.

Line Quality

The speed that information transfers depends on the quality of the phone line. For example, a modem with a speed of 28,800 bps may not reach that speed if the phone line quality is poor.

MODEM

Communications Program

A modem needs a communications program to manage the transmission of information with another modem. This type of program usually comes packaged with a modem.

Handshake

Before exchanging information, modems perform a handshake just as two people shake hands to greet each other. A handshake establishes how the modems will exchange information.

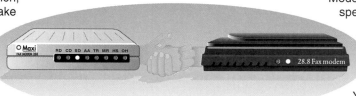

Modems must use the same speed when exchanging information. A fast modem can talk to a slower modem, but they will communicate at the slower speed. You may find that some online services use lower speed modems.

Online

You are online when your modem has successfully connected to another modem. This means the modems are ready and able to exchange information. When your modem is not connected to another modem, you are offline.

DATA COMPRESSION

A modem can compress, or squeeze, data sent to another modem to speed the transfer of data. How much faster the data transfers depends on the type of file being sent. For example, a text file will compress significantly more than a graphics file.

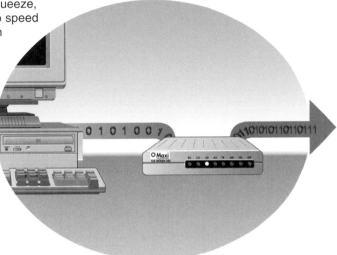

When the information reaches its intended destination, the receiving modem decompresses the information.

ERROR CONTROL

A modem uses error control to ensure that information reliably reaches its destination.

When you send information using a modem, the information is broken down into smaller pieces, called packets. When the packets arrive at the intended destination, the receiving modem checks for damaged packets. If a packet is damaged, the modem that sent the information is asked to send a new copy.

MODEM

MODEM ALTERNATIVES

ISDN

Integrated Services Digital Network (ISDN) is a high-speed digital phone line offered by telephone companies in most urban areas. ISDN is currently the best choice for a high-speed connection to the Internet. ISDN is often used by people working at home who want fast access to information at the office.

ISDN transfers information between the Internet Service Provider (ISP) and your home about four times faster than a modem.

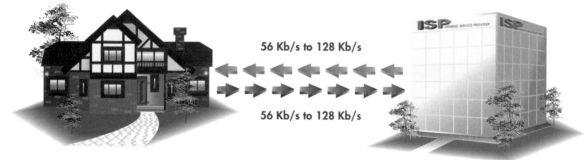

56 Kb/s to 128 Kb/s

56 Kb/s to 128 Kb/s

Cable Modems

A cable modem lets you connect to the Internet with the same cable that attaches to a television set. Cable modems will be offered by many cable companies in the future.

Cable modems transfer information between the Internet Service Provider (ISP) and your home more than 1,000 times faster than a modem.

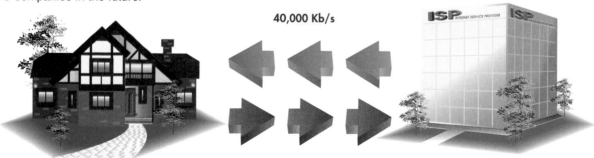

40,000 Kb/s

40,000 Kb/s

ADSL

Asymmetric Digital Subscriber Line (ADSL) is a high-speed digital phone line that will be offered by local telephone companies in the future.

ADSL can send information to your home more than 200 times faster than a modem. ADSL returns information back to the Internet Service Provider (ISP) at a much slower speed.

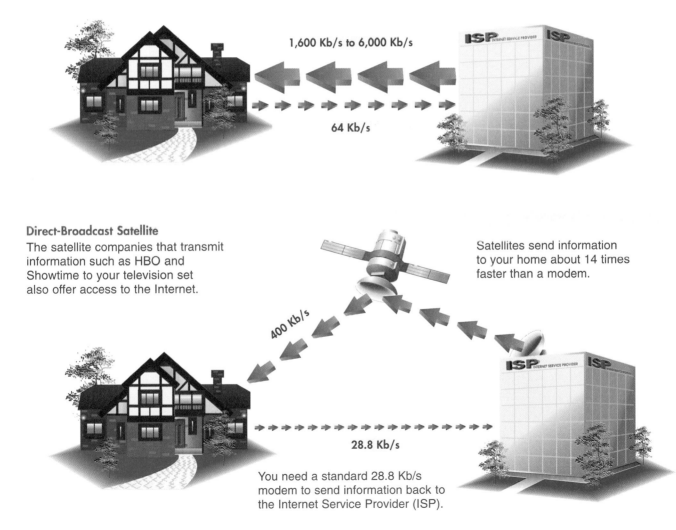

1,600 Kb/s to 6,000 Kb/s

64 Kb/s

Direct-Broadcast Satellite

The satellite companies that transmit information such as HBO and Showtime to your television set also offer access to the Internet.

Satellites send information to your home about 14 times faster than a modem.

400 Kb/s

28.8 Kb/s

You need a standard 28.8 Kb/s modem to send information back to the Internet Service Provider (ISP).

SOUND CARD

A sound card lets a computer play and record high-quality sound.

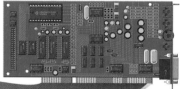

A sound card is a circuit board that plugs into an expansion slot in the computer.

A sound card is also called a sound board or audio card.

Speakers

You need speakers to hear the sound generated by a sound card. Buy speakers with a built-in amplifier between 10 and 30 watts. This will strengthen the sound signal and improve the performance.

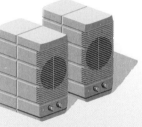

SOUND CARD APPLICATIONS

Games and Multimedia Presentations

A sound card lets you hear music, speech and sound effects during games and multimedia presentations.

Record Sounds

You can use a sound card to record music, speech and sound effects. You can then add the sounds to documents and presentations. You can also use a sound card to compose music on your computer.

SOUND CARD CONNECTIONS

You can see the edge of a sound card
at the back of a computer. A sound card
has a port and several jacks where you
can plug in external devices.

The edge of your sound card may
look different from the sound card
shown here.

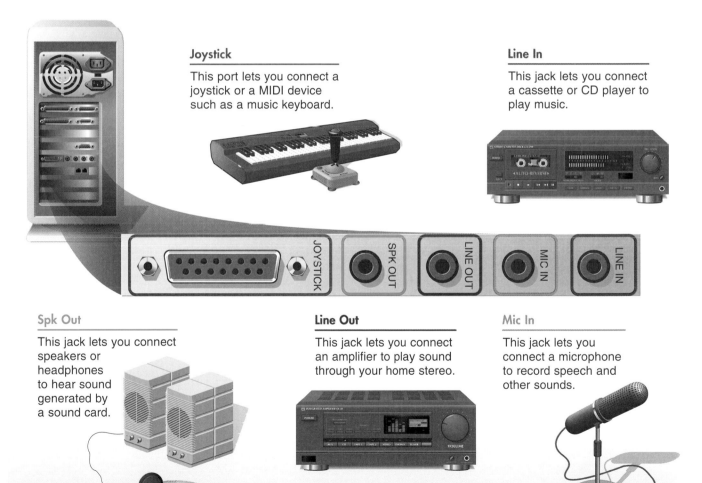

Joystick

This port lets you connect a
joystick or a MIDI device
such as a music keyboard.

Line In

This jack lets you connect
a cassette or CD player to
play music.

Spk Out

This jack lets you connect
speakers or
headphones
to hear sound
generated by
a sound card.

Line Out

This jack lets you connect
an amplifier to play sound
through your home stereo.

Mic In

This jack lets you
connect a microphone
to record speech and
other sounds.

SOUND CARD

Sampling Size and Rate

The sampling size and rate of a sound card determines the quality of the sound produced.

For good sound quality, buy a sound card with a 16-bit sampling size and a 44.1 KHz sampling rate.

If possible, listen to the sounds produced by various sound cards before making your purchase.

Sound Blaster

Make sure you buy a Sound Blaster compatible sound card to ensure your computer has full sound capabilities.

Full-Duplex

A full-duplex sound card lets you talk and listen at the same time. When using a computer to have a conversation over the Internet, a full-duplex sound card lets people talk at the same time. With a half-duplex card, people must take turns talking.

MIDI

Musical Instrument Digital Interface (MIDI) is a set of instructions that allow computers and musical devices to exchange data. This lets you use a computer to play, record and edit music. Many musicians use MIDI to compose music on a computer.

A sound card that supports MIDI ensures that a computer can generate the sounds often found in games, CD-ROM titles and presentation packages.

There are two ways a sound card can produce MIDI sound.

FM Synthesis

FM synthesis imitates the sounds of musical instruments and speech. This results in less realistic sound. FM synthesis is found on low to mid-range sound cards.

Wavetable Synthesis

Wavetable synthesis uses actual recordings of musical instruments and speech. This results in rich, realistic sound. Wavetable synthesis is found on high-quality sound cards.

SCANNER

A scanner is a device that reads graphics and text into a computer.

Scan Graphics

You can scan graphics such as photographs, drawings and logos into a computer. You can then use the graphics in documents, such as reports or newsletters.

Most scanners come with image editing software, which lets you change a scanned graphic.

Scan Text

You can scan text to quickly enter documents into a computer. This lets you scan interesting paper documents and e-mail them to friends or colleagues. You can also scan office documents to store the documents on your computer for quick access.

Most scanners come with Optical Character Recognition (OCR) software. This software places scanned text into a document that can be edited in a word processor.

TYPES OF SCANNERS

Hand-Held Scanner

A hand-held scanner is the least expensive type of scanner. A hand-held scanner has a scanning width of approximately four inches and is ideal for copying small images, such as signatures, logos and small photographs.

Sheet-Fed Scanner

A sheet-fed scanner produces more reliable scans than a hand-held scanner and is less expensive and more compact than a flatbed scanner. A sheet-fed scanner can only scan single sheets of paper. If you want to scan a page from a book, you have to tear out the page.

Flatbed Scanner

A flatbed scanner is the most expensive and most versatile type of scanner. A flatbed scanner is ideal when you want to scan pages from a book without tearing out the pages.

SCANNER

Grayscale Scanner

A grayscale scanner reads images using black, white and shades of gray. A grayscale scanner is ideal for scanning text or when you plan to print scanned images on a black-and-white printer.

Color Scanner

A color scanner is more expensive than a grayscale scanner and reads images using shades of red, blue and green. A color scanner is ideal for scanning images you plan to display in color, such as photographs and illustrations.

Choose the Scanning Mode

When scanning an image, you can choose the scanning mode.

Line Art

The line art mode scans an image using black and white.

Grayscale

The grayscale mode scans an image using black, white and shades of gray.

Color

The color mode scans an image using shades of red, blue and green.

RESOLUTION

The resolution of a scanner determines the amount of detail the scanner can detect.

Scanner resolution is measured in dots per inch (dpi). Some scanners can detect up to 1200 dpi.

Choose the Resolution

Scanning an image at a high resolution results in a clearer, more detailed image, but requires more scanning time and storage space.

20 dpi

72 dpi

300 dpi

You usually do not need to scan an image at a higher resolution than a printer can produce or a monitor can display.

If you plan to print an image on a 300 dpi printer, you do not need to scan at a resolution higher than 300 dpi. Monitors have a maximum resolution of 72 dpi. If you plan to display an image on a monitor, you do not need to scan at a resolution higher than 72 dpi.

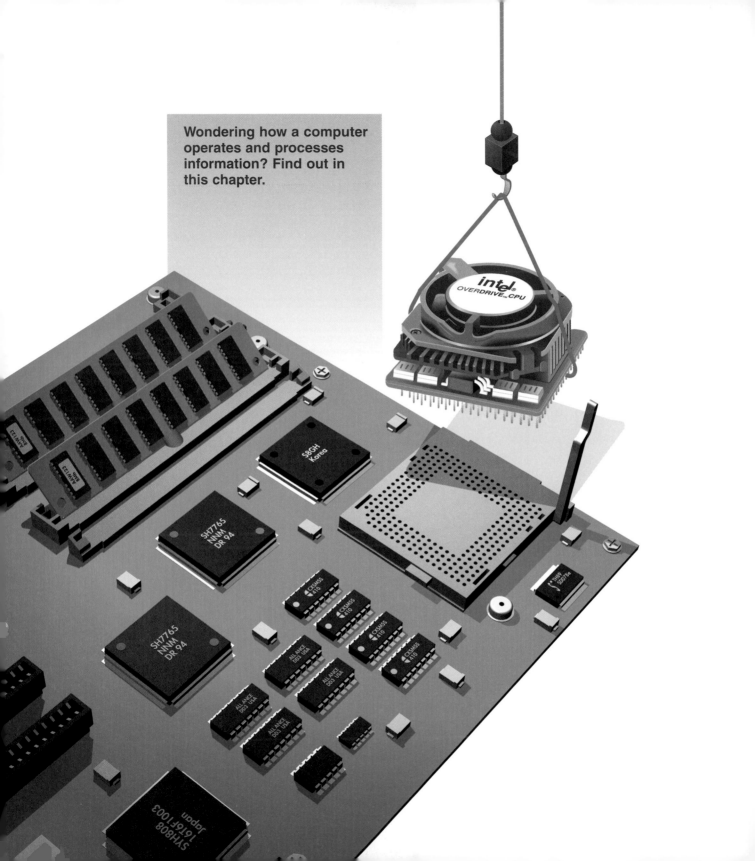

Wondering how a computer operates and processes information? Find out in this chapter.

PROCESSING

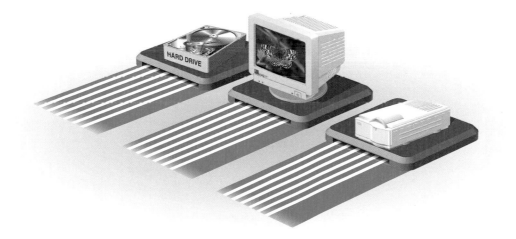

MEMORY

Memory, also called Random Access Memory (RAM), temporarily stores data inside a computer.

Memory works like a blackboard that is constantly overwritten with new data. The data stored in memory disappears when you turn off the computer.

MEMORY SIZE

The amount of memory determines the number of programs a computer can run at once and how fast programs will operate.

Memory is measured in bytes. You should buy a computer with at least 8 MB of memory, but 16 MB is recommended.

You can improve the performance of a computer by adding more memory.

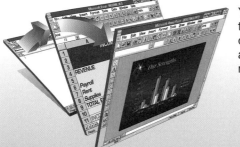

PROGRAM REQUIREMENTS

A program will usually tell you the minimum amount of memory your computer needs to use the program.

System Requirements
- 486 CPU or higher
- Windows 3.1 or higher
- **RAM: 8MB**
- Minimum install: 12 MB
- Monitor: VGA or above
- Mouse or other pointing device

DRAM

Dynamic RAM (DRAM) is a type of memory chip that makes up the main memory in many computer systems.

Extended Data Out DRAM (EDO DRAM) is a faster type of memory chip found in most computer systems.

Synchronous DRAM (SDRAM) is a very fast type of memory chip found in high-end computer systems.

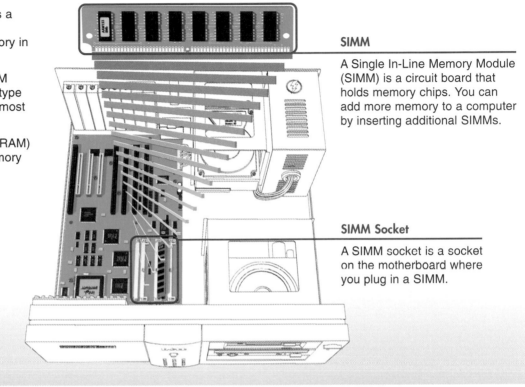

SIMM

A Single In-Line Memory Module (SIMM) is a circuit board that holds memory chips. You can add more memory to a computer by inserting additional SIMMs.

SIMM Socket

A SIMM socket is a socket on the motherboard where you plug in a SIMM.

VIRTUAL MEMORY

If you have limited memory or you have many programs open, your computer may need to use part of the hard drive to simulate more memory.

This simulated memory is called virtual memory and allows the computer to continue operating, but at a much slower speed.

ROM

Unlike RAM, Read-Only Memory (ROM) is permanent and cannot be changed. ROM stores instructions that help prepare the computer for use each time you turn on the computer.

CPU

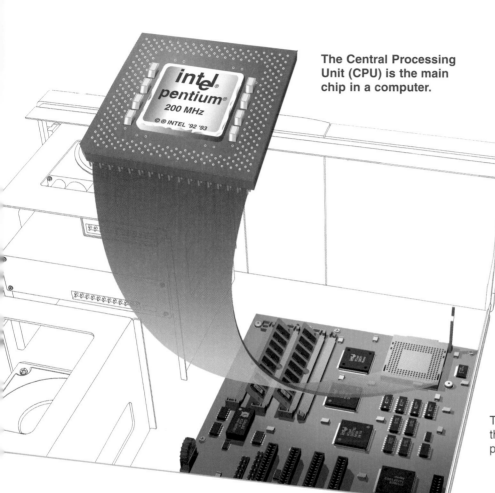

The Central Processing Unit (CPU) is the main chip in a computer.

The CPU processes instructions, performs calculations and manages the flow of information through a computer system. The CPU performs millions of calculations every second.

The CPU is also called the microprocessor or processor.

CPU COMPLEXITY

Imagine a U.S. road map printed on a fingernail and you can imagine the complexity of a CPU. The elements in a CPU can be as small as 0.35 microns wide. By comparison, a human hair is about 100 microns wide.

The manufacturing plants that produce CPUs are tens of thousands of times cleaner than hospital operating rooms. Ultra-sensitive dust filtering systems are needed to eliminate particles that could damage the CPUs.

CHOOSE A CPU

There are several factors that determine the performance of a CPU.

Manufacturer

CPUs for personal computers are made by companies such as Intel, AMD, Cyrix and Motorola. Intel chips are the most popular.

Generation

Each new generation of CPUs is more powerful than the one before. Newer CPUs can process more instructions at a time.

CPU generations include the 486, Pentium (586) and Pentium Pro (686). The older 386 generation is obsolete.

Speed

Each CPU generation is available in several speeds. The CPU speed is a major factor in determining how fast a computer operates. The faster the speed, the faster the computer operates.

The speed of a CPU is measured in megahertz (MHz), or millions of cycles per second.

CPU

486

Older computers use the 486 chip. There are four types of 486 chips.

486SX	Does not include a math coprocessor.
486DX	Includes a math coprocessor to speed the performance of complex math calculations.
486DX2	Performs twice as fast as the 486DX.
486DX4	Performs three times as fast as the 486DX.

Pentium

The Pentium chip is ideal for computers using Windows 3.1 and Windows 95. Pentium chips are available with speeds of 75, 100, 133, 166 and 200 MHz.

When buying a new computer, do not consider anything less than a Pentium chip.

Pentium Pro

The Pentium Pro chip is ideal for computers that use powerful operating systems such as Windows NT and Unix.

Pentium Pro chips are available with speeds of 150, 166, 180 and 200 MHz.

Intel plans to add multimedia extensions (MMX) to the Pentium and Pentium Pro chips. This will dramatically improve the performance of multimedia tasks such as the processing of graphics, video and sound.

UPGRADE A CPU

You can increase the processing
power of a computer by replacing
the CPU chip with a new one.

OverDrive Chip

An OverDrive chip replaces the
existing CPU chip in a computer.
An OverDrive chip lets you
improve the performance of
your computer without having
to buy a new computer.

You cannot upgrade all CPU chips.
Even if you can upgrade an old
chip, the rest of your computer
may not be fast enough to make
it worthwhile. In this situation,
the best solution is to buy a
new computer.

ZIF Socket

A Zero Insertion Force (ZIF)
socket lets you easily remove
and then replace the CPU.

You remove the chip by
raising the tiny handle that
secures the chip. After raising
the handle, you can easily lift
out the chip and replace it
with a new one.

MEMORY CACHE

Memory cache speeds up the computer by storing data the computer has recently used.

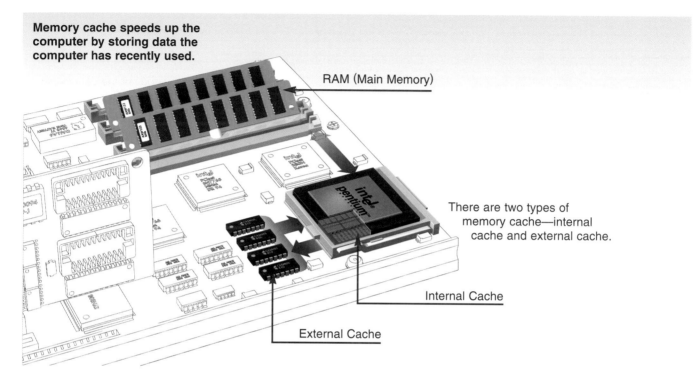

RAM (Main Memory)

There are two types of memory cache—internal cache and external cache.

Internal Cache

External Cache

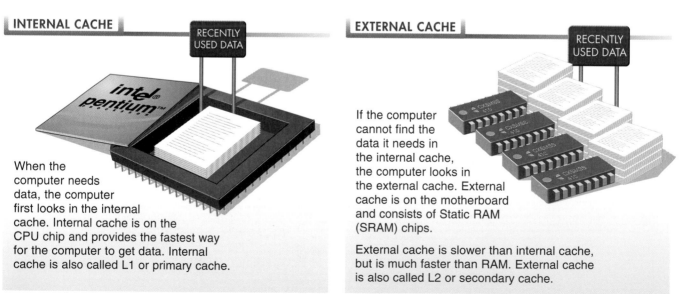

INTERNAL CACHE

RECENTLY USED DATA

When the computer needs data, the computer first looks in the internal cache. Internal cache is on the CPU chip and provides the fastest way for the computer to get data. Internal cache is also called L1 or primary cache.

EXTERNAL CACHE

RECENTLY USED DATA

If the computer cannot find the data it needs in the internal cache, the computer looks in the external cache. External cache is on the motherboard and consists of Static RAM (SRAM) chips.

External cache is slower than internal cache, but is much faster than RAM. External cache is also called L2 or secondary cache.

RAM

If the computer cannot find the data it needs in the internal or external cache, the computer must get the data from the slower main memory, called RAM.

Each time the computer requests data from RAM, the computer places a copy of the data in the memory cache. This process constantly updates the memory cache so it always contains the most recently used data.

USING MEMORY CACHE

Using memory cache is similar to working with documents in your office. When you need information, you look for information in a specific order. Each step along the way takes up more of your valuable time.

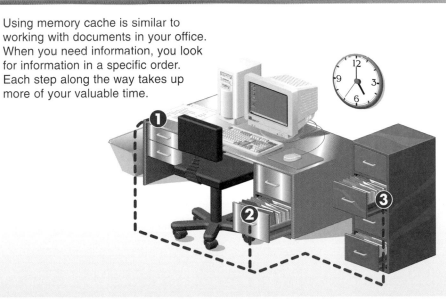

❶ Look through documents on your desk (internal cache).

❷ Look through documents in your desk drawer (external cache).

❸ Look through documents in your filing cabinet (RAM).

Working without memory cache would be similar to looking through the filing cabinet each time you need a document.

BUS

The bus is the electronic pathway in a computer that carries information between devices.

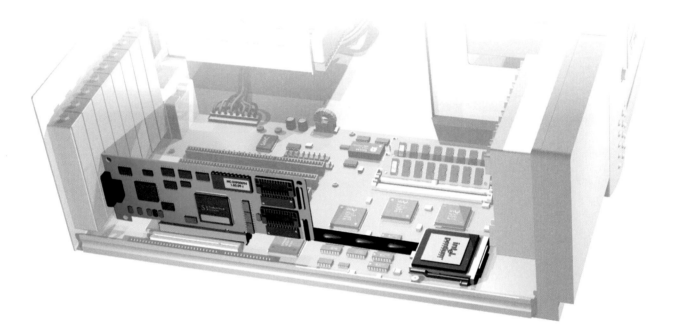

Bus Width

The bus width is similar to the number of lanes on a highway. The greater the width, the more data can flow along the bus at a time. Bus width is measured in bits. Eight bits equals one character.

Bus Speed

The bus speed is similar to the speed limit on a highway. The higher the speed, the faster data travels along the bus. Bus speed is measured in megahertz (MHz), or millions of cycles per second.

66 MHz

TYPES OF BUSES

ISA Bus

The Industry Standard Architecture (ISA) bus is the slowest and oldest type of bus. This bus is ideal for transferring information to and from a slow device, such as a modem. The ISA bus has a width of 16 bits and a speed of 8 MHz.

The ISA bus is found in 486, Pentium and Pentium Pro computers.

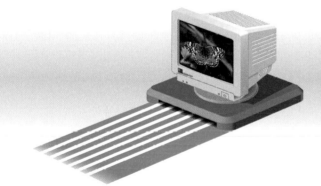

VL-Bus

The Video Local Bus (VL-Bus) transfers information much faster than the ISA bus. This bus is primarily used to send data to a monitor. The VL-Bus has a width of 32 bits and speeds of up to 40 MHz.

The VL-Bus is found in 486 computers.

PCI Bus

The Peripheral Component Interconnect (PCI) bus is the most sophisticated type of bus. This bus can handle many high-speed devices. The PCI bus can have a width of 32 or 64 bits and speeds of up to 66 MHz.

The PCI bus is found in Pentium and Pentium Pro computers.

The PCI bus supports Plug and Play, which lets you add new devices to a computer without complex installation procedures.

What is a hard drive? What does a CD-ROM drive do? Learn about storage devices in this chapter.

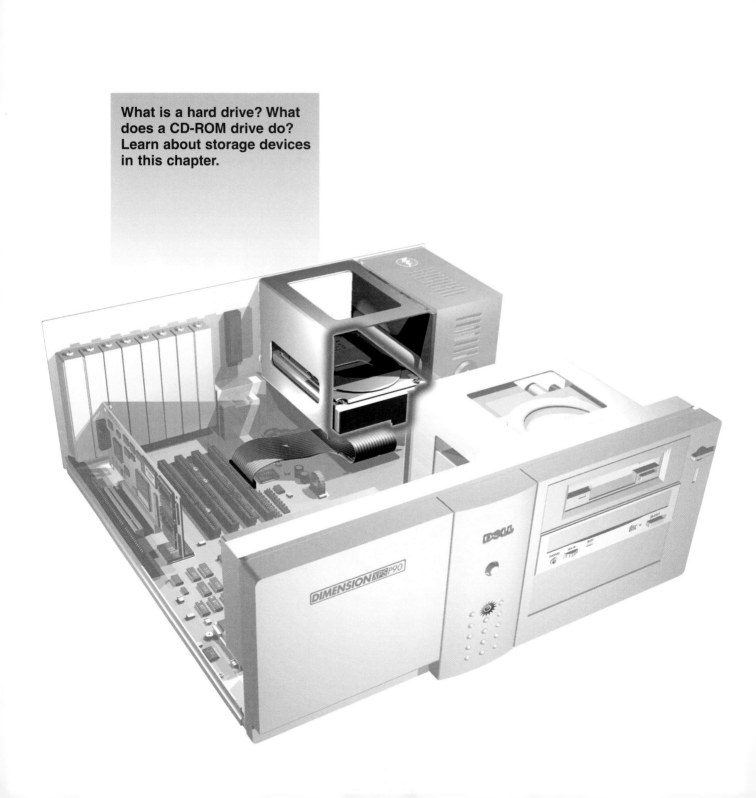

STORAGE DEVICES

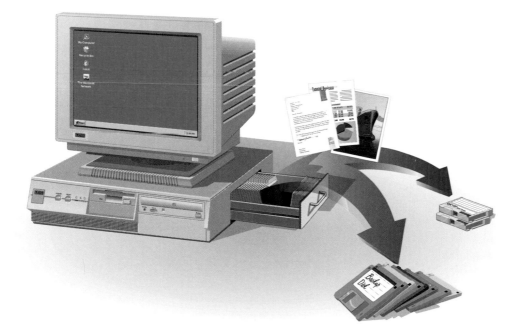

HARD DRIVE

The hard drive is the primary device that a computer uses to store information.

Most computers have one hard drive, located inside the computer case. If a computer has one hard drive, it is called drive C. If a computer has additional hard drives, they are called drives D, E, F, and so on.

The hard drive is also called the hard disk, hard disk drive or fixed disk drive.

The hard drive light is on when the computer is using the hard drive. Do not move the computer when this light is on.

Inside a Hard Drive
The hard drive magnetically stores data on a stack of rotating disks, called platters.

A hard drive has several read/write heads that read and record data on the disks.

HARD DRIVE CONTENTS

Program Files

A hard drive stores your programs. When you buy a new program, you must install, or copy, the program files to your hard drive before you can use the program.

Data Files

A hard drive stores your data files such as documents, spreadsheets and graphics.

Programs come on a CD-ROM disc or several floppy disks.

STORE FILES

Save Files

When you are creating a document, the computer stores the document in temporary memory. If you want to store a document for future use, you must save the document to the hard drive. If you do not save the document, the document will be lost when there is a power failure or you turn off the computer.

Organize Files

Like a filing cabinet, a hard drive uses folders or directories to organize information.

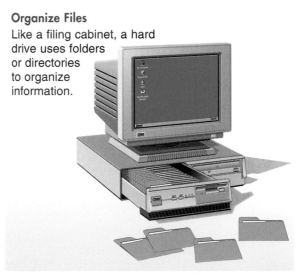

HARD DRIVE

CHOOSE A HARD DRIVE

Capacity

The amount of information a hard drive can store is measured in bytes.

A hard drive with a capacity of 850 MB to 1.2 GB will suit most home and business users.

Purchase the largest hard drive you can afford. New programs and data will quickly fill a hard drive. For example, Microsoft Word is a word processing program that requires about 16 MB of hard drive space. Windows 95 is an operating system that requires about 40 MB.

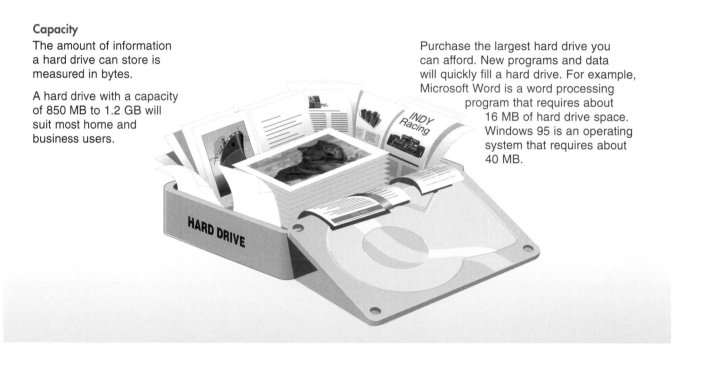

Average Access Time

The average access time is the speed at which a hard drive finds data.

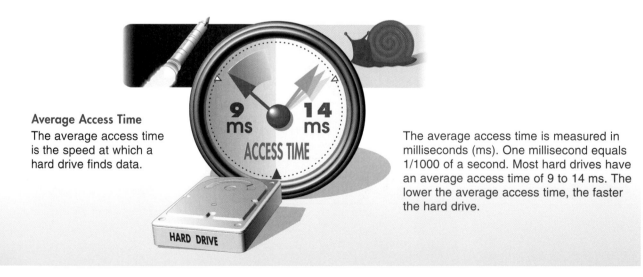

The average access time is measured in milliseconds (ms). One millisecond equals 1/1000 of a second. Most hard drives have an average access time of 9 to 14 ms. The lower the average access time, the faster the hard drive.

CONNECTION TYPE

IDE

Integrated Drive Electronics (IDE) is the least expensive way to connect a hard drive to a computer.

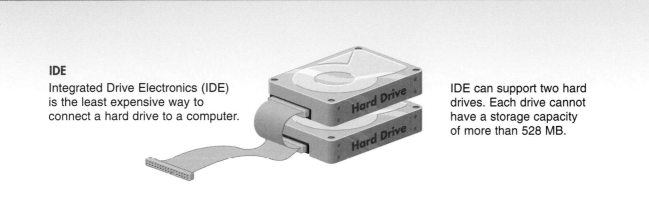

IDE can support two hard drives. Each drive cannot have a storage capacity of more than 528 MB.

EIDE

Most new computers come with Enhanced IDE (EIDE). EIDE is faster and can connect more devices to a computer than IDE.

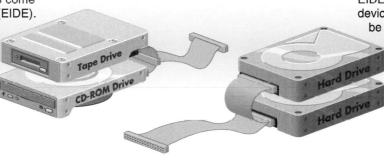

EIDE can support up to four devices. These devices can be hard drives with storage capacities over 528 MB, or other devices such as CD-ROM and tape drives.

SCSI

Small Computer System Interface (SCSI) is the fastest, most flexible, but most expensive way to connect a hard drive and other devices to a computer. SCSI is pronounced "scuzzy."

SCSI can connect up to seven devices. These devices can include removable hard drives, CD-ROM drives, tape drives, scanners and printers.

HARD DRIVE

Removable hard drives are available. Popular removable hard drives include Jaz and Zip drives.

A Jaz drive can store up to 1 GB (1,000 MB) of data, whereas a Zip drive can store 100 MB of data.

Archive Data

You can use a removable hard drive to store old or rarely used files. You can then remove the files from your computer to provide more storage space.

Protect Data

You can use a removable hard drive to store confidential information or backup copies of data. You can then protect the data by placing the disks in a safe place on nights and weekends.

Transfer Data

You can use a removable hard drive to transfer large amounts of information between computers. For example, you can take work home or transfer information to a colleague.

DISK CACHE

The disk cache speeds up the computer by storing data the computer has recently used.

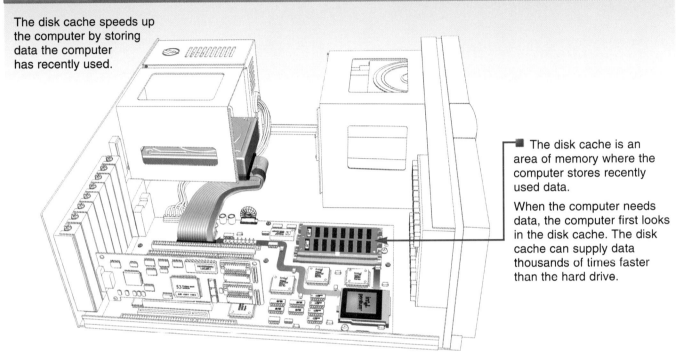

■ The disk cache is an area of memory where the computer stores recently used data.

When the computer needs data, the computer first looks in the disk cache. The disk cache can supply data thousands of times faster than the hard drive.

If the computer cannot find the data it needs in the disk cache, the computer looks on the hard drive.

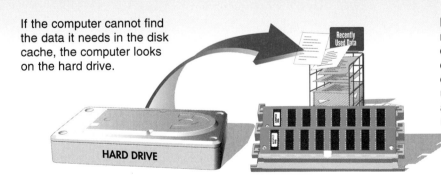

Each time the computer requests data from the hard drive, the computer places a copy of the data in the disk cache. This process constantly updates the disk cache so it always contains the most recently used data.

HARD DRIVE

Defragment a Drive

A fragmented hard drive stores parts of a file in many different locations. To retrieve a file, the computer must search many areas of the drive.

You can use a defragmentation program to place all parts of a file in one location. This reduces the time the hard drive spends locating the file.

Defragmenting your hard drive once a month can improve the performance of the computer.

Windows 95 includes a defragmentation program called Defragmenter.

Repair a Drive

You can improve the performance of a computer by using a disk repair program to search for and repair disk errors. You should check a hard drive for errors at least once a month.

Windows 95 includes a disk repair program called ScanDisk.

CREATE MORE DISK SPACE

Archive Information

Store old or rarely used files on a tape cartridge, removable hard disk or floppy disks. You can then remove the files from your computer to provide more storage space.

Delete Files

Delete all files and programs you no longer need from your computer. Clean up a hard drive as you would clean up old documents stored in a filing cabinet.

Data Compression

You can compress, or squeeze together, the files stored on a hard drive. This can double the amount of information the drive can store.

You should only compress a hard drive if it is running out of space to store new information and you have tried all other ways of increasing the available storage space.

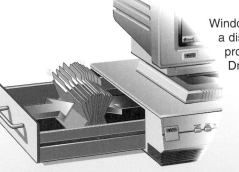

Windows 95 includes a disk compression program called DriveSpace.

HARD DRIVE

Virus

A virus is a program that disrupts the normal operation of a computer. A virus can cause a variety of problems, such as the appearance of annoying messages on the screen or the destruction of information on the hard drive.

Floppy Disk

If you receive files on a floppy disk from a colleague or friend, make sure you check for viruses before using the files. Never start your computer when the floppy drive contains a disk that you have not checked for viruses.

Modem

Files you receive through a modem may contain viruses. Make sure you check for viruses before using any files you receive through a modem.

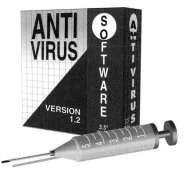

Anti-Virus Programs

You should regularly use an anti-virus program to check for viruses on your computer. Most computer stores offer anti-virus programs. You can also get anti-virus programs on the Internet. Make sure you update your anti-virus programs since new viruses are being discovered every day.

Back Up Data

You should copy the files stored on your hard drive to floppy disks or tape cartridges. This provides extra copies in case the original files are stolen or damaged due to viruses or computer failure.

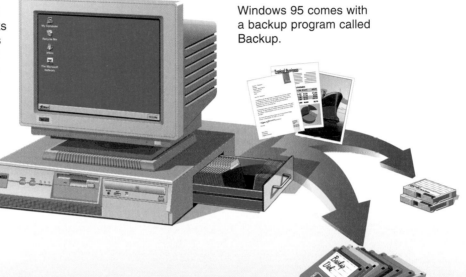

Windows 95 comes with a backup program called Backup.

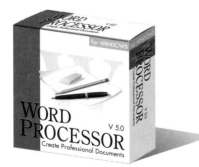

Back Up Work

You only need to back up your own work. You do not need to back up programs stored on your computer since you can use the original program disks to re-install the programs. Make sure you keep the program disks in a safe place.

Back Up Frequently

Consider how much work you can afford to lose. If you can afford to lose the work accomplished in one day, back up once a day. If your work does not often change during the week, back up once a week.

Create and then strictly follow a backup schedule. Hard drive disasters always seem to happen right after you miss a scheduled backup.

FLOPPY DRIVE

A floppy drive stores and retrieves information on floppy disks.

A computer has one or two floppy drives. If a computer has one floppy drive, the drive is called drive A. If a computer has two floppy drives, the second drive is called drive B.

A floppy drive stores information on floppy disks, or diskettes. A floppy disk is a removable device that magnetically stores data.

TYPES OF FLOPPY DISKS

3.5 Inch Floppy Disk

Most floppy drives use 3.5 inch floppy disks. Inside a 3.5 inch floppy disk is a thin, plastic, flexible disk that magnetically records information. The word floppy refers to this flexible disk.

5.25 Inch Floppy Disk

Older computers use 5.25 inch floppy disks.

FLOPPY DISK APPLICATIONS

Install New Programs

Programs you buy at a computer store can come on one or several floppy disks. Before you can use a program, you must install, or copy, the contents of the floppy disks onto your computer.

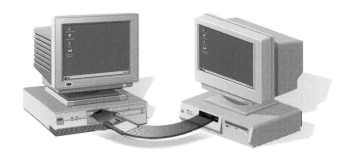

Transfer Data

You can use floppy disks to transfer data from one computer to another. This lets you give data to friends and colleagues.

Back Up Data

You can protect the files stored on a computer by copying the files to floppy disks. These files will serve as backup copies if your hard drive fails or you accidentally erase important files.

Increase Hard Drive Space

You can increase the available space on your computer by copying old or rarely used files to floppy disks. You can then remove the files from the computer to provide more storage space.

FLOPPY DRIVE

INSERT A FLOPPY DISK

Push the floppy disk gently into the drive, label side up. Most drives make a "click" sound when you have fully inserted the disk.

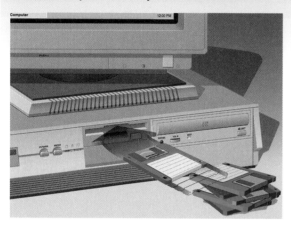

■ This light is on when the computer is using the floppy disk. Do not remove the disk when this light is on.

■ To remove the floppy disk, press this button.

PROTECT A FLOPPY DISK

You can prevent erasing and recording information on a floppy disk by sliding the tab to the write-protected position.

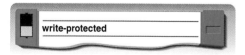

You **cannot** erase and record information.

You **can** erase and record information.

Make sure you keep floppy disks away from magnets, which can damage the information stored on the disks. Also make sure you do not store floppy disks in extremely hot or cold locations and try not to spill liquids such as coffee or soda on the disks.

CHOOSE A FLOPPY DISK

Floppy Disk Capacity
Floppy disks come in two storage capacities. High-density disks store more information than double-density disks.

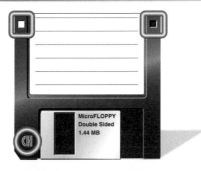

Double-Density
A double-density (DD) floppy disk can store 720 K of information. This disk has only one hole at the top of the disk.

High-Density
A high-density (HD) floppy disk can store 1.44 MB of information. This disk has two holes at the top of the disk and usually displays the letters HD.

Formatted Floppy Disk
A floppy disk must be formatted before you can use it to store data. Formatting a disk prepares the disk for use by dividing it into tracks and sectors. This organizes the disk so the computer can store and retrieve information.

You can save time by purchasing ready-to-use, formatted floppy disks.

Double-Sided Floppy Disk
A double-sided (DS) floppy disk stores data on both sides of the disk. Older, single-sided (SS) disks stored data on only one side of the disk.

CD-ROM DRIVE

A CD-ROM drive is a device that reads information stored on compact discs.

Most CD-ROM drives are located inside the computer case. External CD-ROM drives that connect to the computer by a cable are also available.

CD-ROM DISC

A CD-ROM disc is the same type of disc you buy at a music store.

A single CD-ROM disc can store more than 600 MB of data. This is equal to an entire set of encyclopedias or over 400 floppy disks. The large storage capacity of CD-ROM discs leaves more room for storing large images, animation and video.

CD-ROM stands for Compact Disc-Read Only Memory. Read-only means you cannot change the information stored on a disc.

CD-ROM APPLICATIONS

Install Programs
The large storage capacity of a CD-ROM disc makes installing new programs on your computer easy. A program that requires twenty floppy disks can easily fit on a single CD-ROM disc.

Play CD-ROM Titles
There are thousands of educational and entertaining CD-ROM discs available. Most CD-ROM titles are interactive. You can move through topics covered on a disc at your own pace and find topics of interest in seconds.

Play Music CDs
You can play music CDs on a CD-ROM drive while you work.

CD-ROM DRIVE

A CD-ROM disc can store multimedia presentations.

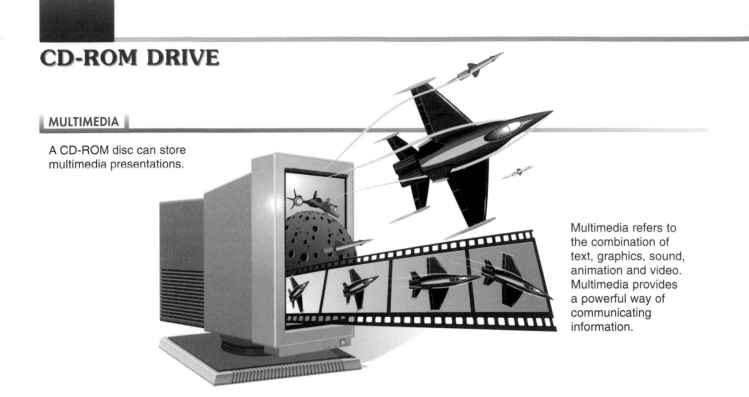

Multimedia refers to the combination of text, graphics, sound, animation and video. Multimedia provides a powerful way of communicating information.

There are thousands of multimedia titles available to inform and entertain you. You can buy multimedia titles at most computer stores.

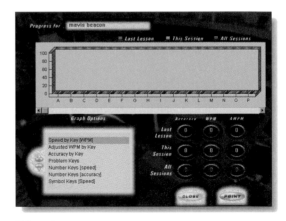

Children

Hundreds of multimedia titles are available to stimulate a child's imagination. There are stories that offer magical adventures and games for children of all ages. Many games teach basic skills such as reading, writing, spelling and math.

Education

There are many stimulating and comprehensive educational titles that can teach you new skills. You can learn how to type, renovate your home or speak a new language.

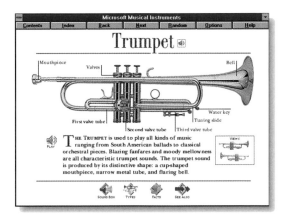

Games

Multimedia games can keep you entertained for hours. You can defend your world from invading aliens, play golf or football, try to defeat the dealer in a blackjack game or enjoy the sights and sounds of real flight.

General Interest

You can use multimedia titles to explore the world around you. Learn about the instruments in an orchestra, discover how to treat common illnesses, stroll through an art gallery or take a trip through the solar system.

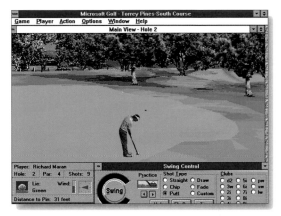

Reference

CD-ROM discs that store large collections of information, such as encyclopedias, maps, magazine articles and dictionaries, are available. You can instantly search for information stored on a disc.

Time-Sensitive Discs

Some CD-ROM discs, such as a disc containing telephone numbers, are time-sensitive and will soon become outdated.

If you need the information to be up-to-date, ask the manufacturer for updated versions of the disc. Some CD-ROM titles, such as Microsoft Encarta, let you access updated information on the Internet.

CD-ROM DRIVE

CHOOSE A CD-ROM DRIVE

Speed

The speed of a CD-ROM drive determines how fast a disc spins. With faster speeds, a disc can transfer information to the computer more quickly, which results in better performance.

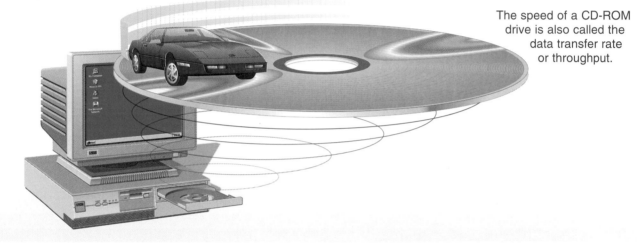

The speed of a CD-ROM drive is also called the data transfer rate or throughput.

Speed is very important when viewing video and animation often found in games and encyclopedias. Slow speeds will result in jerky performances.

Single (1x)	150 Kb/s
Double (2x)	300 Kb/s
Triple (3x)	450 Kb/s
Quad (4x)	600 Kb/s
Six (6x)	900 Kb/s
Eight (8x)	1,200 Kb/s

These are the available speeds. You should buy a CD-ROM drive with a speed of at least 600 Kb/s.

Average Access Time

The average access time indicates how quickly a CD-ROM drive can find information stored on a disc. Average access times typically range from 150 ms to 300 ms.

The lower the average access time, the quicker you can find what you are looking for on a disc containing large amounts of information.

Multisession

Information can be stored on a disc at several different times, called sessions. For example, with a Photo CD, you can have a photo finisher record slides on a disc and then add more slides to the disc at a later date.

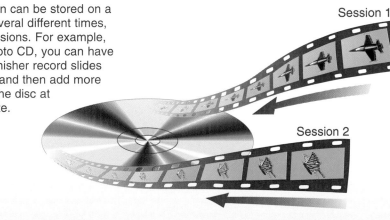

Older, single session CD-ROM drives can only read the original data recorded on a disc. Multisession CD-ROM drives can read both the original data and the data that was later added to the disc.

CD-ROM DRIVE

Insert a Disc

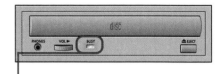

■ This light is on when the CD-ROM drive is accessing information on the disc. Do not remove the disc or move the computer when this light is on.

■ To insert or remove a disc, press this button.

■ A tray slides out. Place the disc, label side up, on the tray. To close the tray, press the button again.

Headphones

You can use headphones to listen to recorded sounds on a disc. Headphones are useful in noisy environments or when you want to listen to a disc privately.

Handling Discs

When handling a CD-ROM disc, hold the disc around the edges.

Protecting Discs

When you finish using a disc, make sure you place the disc back in its protective case. Do not stack discs on top of each other.

CD-ROM ALTERNATIVES

CD-Recordable

CD-Recordable (CD-R) drives are available if you want to store your own information on discs. These drives are often used to back up hard drives or to distribute and archive information.

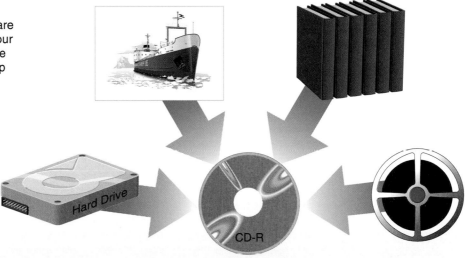

DVD-ROM

The Digital Video Disc-ROM (DVD-ROM) drive is similar to a CD-ROM drive. A DVD-ROM disc has a storage capacity starting at 4.7 GB, which equals over six CD-ROM discs.

DVD-ROM

A DVD-ROM disc can hold a two hour, full-screen movie with better quality than a VHS tape.

CD-ROM

A DVD-ROM drive is able to read your CD-ROM discs.

TAPE DRIVE

A tape drive is a device that copies the files stored on a computer onto tape cartridges.

Tape drives are also called tape backup units.

A tape drive can be inside the computer case or connected to the computer by a cable. An external tape drive is more expensive, but you can use it with more than one computer.

Tape Cartridges

A tape drive stores information on tape cartridges. These cartridges are similar to the cassettes you buy at music stores.

Store all cartridges in a cool, dry place, away from electrical equipment.

TAPE DRIVE APPLICATIONS

Back Up Data

Most people use tape drives to make backup copies of files stored on a computer. This provides extra copies in case the original files are stolen or damaged due to viruses or computer failure. Most people should back up their work every day.

Archive Data

You can copy old or rarely used files from your computer to tape cartridges. You can then remove the files from your computer to provide more storage space.

Transfer Data

You can use a tape drive to transfer large amounts of information between computers. Make sure the person receiving the information uses the same type of tape drive.

TAPE DRIVE

A backup program helps you copy the files stored on your computer to tape cartridges.

Most tape drives come with a backup program specifically designed for use with the drive. Windows 95 also includes a backup program.

Schedule Backups

You can set a backup program to run automatically. This lets you schedule a backup at night, when you are not using your computer.

Types of Backups

A full backup will back up all your files. An incremental backup will back up only the files that have changed since the last backup. An incremental backup saves you time when backing up a lot of information.

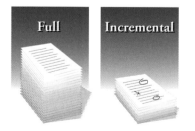

Compress Data

A backup program can compress, or squeeze, data you are backing up to double the amount of data you can store on a tape cartridge.

TYPES OF TAPE DRIVES

QIC Drive

A Quarter-Inch Cartridge (QIC) drive is currently the most common type of tape drive. A high-quality QIC drive can store up to 4 GB of data.

Travan Drive

Travan is a new type of tape drive. This drive stores more information and is faster than a QIC drive. A Travan drive also accepts QIC tape cartridges. A high-quality Travan drive can store up to 8 GB of data.

DAT Drive

A Digital Audio Tape (DAT) drive is the fastest, most reliable, but most expensive type of tape drive. A high-quality DAT drive can store up to 10 GB of data.

TAPE CARTRIDGE TIP

Companies often advertise the amount of compressed data a tape cartridge can store. Companies assume that compression will double the amount of information a cartridge can store. This is not always the case.

The amount of information that is actually compressed depends on the type of information you are backing up. For example, a text file will compress significantly more than a graphics file.

Wondering what to look for in a portable computer? This chapter will provide all the information you need.

CHAPTER 5:

PORTABLE COMPUTERS

INTRODUCTION TO PORTABLE COMPUTERS

A portable is a small, lightweight computer that you can easily transport.

A portable computer is also called a laptop or notebook.

You can buy a portable computer with the same capabilities as a desktop computer, although portable computers are more expensive.

A portable computer has a built-in keyboard, pointing device and screen. This eliminates the need for cables to connect these devices to the portable.

ADVANTAGES OF PORTABLES

Travel

A portable computer lets you work when traveling or outdoors. You can also use a portable computer to bring work home instead of staying late at the office.

Presentations

You can bring a portable computer to meetings to present information.

BATTERY

A battery or an electrical outlet can supply the power for a portable computer.

A battery lets you use a portable when no electrical outlets are available.

TYPES OF BATTERIES

There are two main types of batteries—nickel metal hydride (NiMH) and lithium-ion. Lithium-ion is a more expensive, newer battery that is lighter and lasts longer than NiMH.

RECHARGE A BATTERY

The power supplied by a battery lasts for only a few hours. You must recharge a battery before you can use it again. If you are unable to recharge a battery when traveling, bring an extra battery so you can work for a longer period of time.

MONITOR A BATTERY

Most portables display the amount of battery power remaining, either on the screen or on a panel built into the computer.

SCREEN

The screen on a portable computer uses liquid crystal display (LCD). This is the same type of display found in most digital wristwatches.

An LCD screen uses very little electricity, which extends the length of time you can use a battery before needing to recharge. An LCD screen also weighs much less than a desktop monitor, which makes a portable easier to carry.

BACKLIGHT

Most portables have an internal light source at the back of the screen. This makes the screen easier to view in poorly lit areas but shortens the length of time you can use a battery before needing to recharge.

SCREEN SIZE

The size of the screen is measured diagonally. Screen sizes range from about 9 to 12 inches.

POWER A FULL-SIZE MONITOR

Most portables can power both the portable screen and a full-size monitor at the same time. This feature is very useful when delivering presentations.

TYPES OF SCREENS

Passive Matrix

This type of screen is less expensive than an active matrix screen, but is not as bright or rich in color. The lower cost makes a passive matrix screen ideal for routine office tasks.

Dual-scan passive matrix screens are brighter and richer in color than the older, single-scan passive matrix screens.

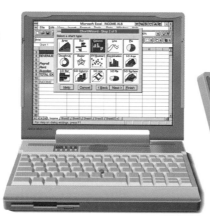

A passive matrix screen is also called a Double SuperTwisted Nematic (DSTN) screen.

Passive matrix screens can be difficult to read when viewed from an angle. This is ideal when you want to keep work private from people sitting next to you on a train or plane, but makes delivering a presentation to several people difficult.

Active Matrix

This type of screen is more expensive, but displays brighter, richer colors than a passive matrix screen.

An active matrix screen is also called a Thin-Film Transistor (TFT) screen.

You can view an active matrix screen from wide angles, which makes it more suitable for delivering presentations to several people.

INPUT AND OUTPUT DEVICES

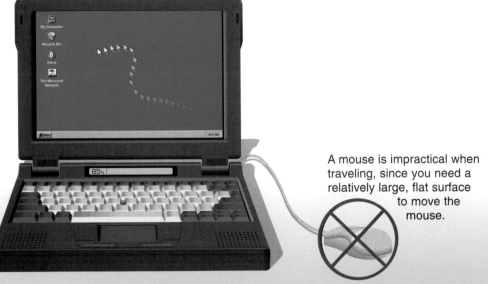

There are several devices that let you move the pointer around the screen of a portable computer.

A mouse is impractical when traveling, since you need a relatively large, flat surface to move the mouse.

Pointing Stick

Many portables have a small, eraser-like device that you push in different directions to move the pointer on the screen.

Trackball

A trackball is an upside-down mouse that remains stationary. You roll the ball with your fingers or palm to move the pointer on the screen. Built-in trackballs on the right side of the keyboard may be awkward for left-handed users.

Touchpad

A touchpad is a surface that is sensitive to pressure and motion. When you move your fingertip across the pad, the pointer on the screen moves in the same direction.

KEYBOARD

The keys on a portable keyboard may be small and close together to save space. Before buying a portable, type several paragraphs of text to make sure the keyboard is suitable for you.

Some portable computers have a keyboard that expands to a full-size keyboard.

MODEM

You can buy a portable with a built-in modem or add modem capabilities later. When traveling, a modem lets you connect to the network at work to exchange messages and files.

Many hotel phone systems cannot support modems. Check with hotel management before using your modem.

SOUND CARD AND SPEAKERS

You can buy a portable with a built-in sound card and speakers to play and record sound. This is very useful when you want to use the portable to deliver presentations.

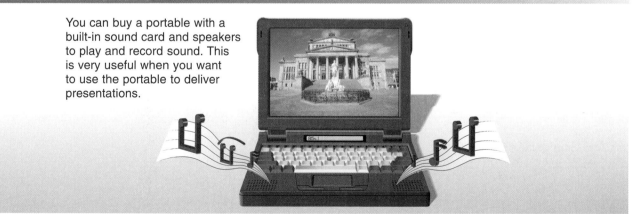

STORAGE DEVICES

HARD DRIVE

The hard drive is the primary device a portable uses to store information. Buy the largest hard drive you can afford. New programs and data will quickly fill a hard drive.

FLOPPY DRIVE

Many portables come with a floppy drive to store and retrieve information on floppy disks.

If you will not often use a floppy drive, you can buy a portable without a floppy drive to reduce the portable's weight. You can then connect the portable to an external floppy drive when necessary.

CD-ROM DRIVE

A portable computer may come with a CD-ROM drive to read information stored on compact discs.

Some portables let you replace the CD-ROM drive with another component. These components can include an extra battery to increase the amount of time you can use the portable, a second hard drive for additional storage space or a floppy drive.

PROCESSING

CPU

The Central Processing Unit (CPU) is the main chip in a computer. The CPU processes instructions, performs calculations and manages the flow of information through a computer system.

CPU	SPEED (MHz)
486DX2	66
486DX4	75 100
Pentium	75 90 100 120 133

This chart shows the CPU chips available for portable computers. Which chip you decide to buy depends on your budget and how you plan to use the computer.

MEMORY

Electronic memory, or RAM, temporarily stores data inside a computer. Memory works like a blackboard that is constantly overwritten with new data. A portable computer running Windows 95 needs at least 8 MB of memory to ensure that programs run smoothly.

PCMCIA CARD

A PCMCIA Card adds a new capability, such as sound or additional memory, to a portable computer.

Some PCMCIA Cards provide multiple features. For example, a single PCMCIA Card can provide networking and modem capabilities.

PCMCIA stands for Personal Computer Memory Card International Association. A PCMCIA Card is also called a PC Card.

TYPES OF PCMCIA CARDS

A PCMCIA Card is a lightweight device about the size of a credit card. There are three types of PCMCIA Cards—Type I, Type II and Type III. Type I is the thinnest card, while Type III is the thickest.

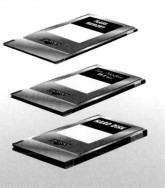

PCMCIA SLOT

You insert a PCMCIA Card into a slot on a portable computer. Most portable computers have a PCMCIA slot that can accept a Type II or a Type III PCMCIA Card.

USE A PORTABLE AT WORK

Port Replicator

A port replicator lets you connect many devices, such as a printer, modem and mouse, to a portable at once. After you connect a portable to a port replicator, you can use all the devices attached to the port replicator without having to attach each device individually.

Docking Station

A docking station lets you connect many devices to a portable at once. A docking station can also provide additional features, such as a CD-ROM drive, networking capabilities and full-sized monitor and keyboard.

After you connect a portable to a docking station, you can use all the features found on the docking station.

Infrared Port

Some portable computers have an infrared port to share information without using cables to physically connect to another computer or device. Infrared ports are commonly used for connecting a portable computer to a printer or network.

Ready to start that report? Browse through this chapter to discover how application software can help you get the job done.

CHAPTER 6

APPLICATION SOFTWARE

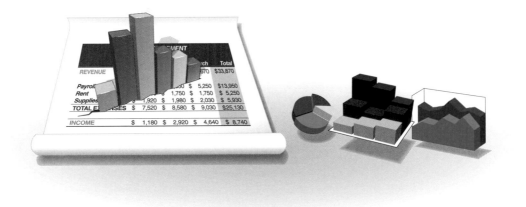

INTRODUCTION TO APPLICATION SOFTWARE

Application software helps you accomplish specific tasks.

You can use application software to write letters, manage your finances, draw pictures, play games and much more.

Application software is also called software, an application or a program.

SOFTWARE VERSION

Software developers and manufacturers constantly make corrections (called bug-fixes) and add new features to the software they create. When a manufacturer releases updated software, the software is given a new version number. This helps people distinguish new versions of the software from older versions.

BUNDLED SOFTWARE

Bundled software is software that comes with a new computer system or device, such as a printer. Companies often include bundled software to let you start using the new equipment right away. For example, new computer systems usually come with word processing, spreadsheet and graphics programs.

GET HELP

Most software comes with a built-in help feature and printed documentation to help you learn to use the software. You can also buy computer books with detailed, step-by-step instructions at computer or book stores.

WORD PROCESSOR

A word processor helps you create professional-looking documents quickly and efficiently.

Popular word processing programs include Microsoft Word, Corel WordPerfect and Lotus Word Pro.

WORD PROCESSING HIGHLIGHTS

Documents

You can create documents such as letters, reports, manuals, newsletters and brochures. You can style documents to make them attractive or add pictures.

Tables

You can create tables to organize information. You can also add colors and borders to enhance the appearance of tables.

Mail Merge

Word processors offer a merge feature that lets you quickly produce personalized letters, envelopes and mailing labels for each person on a mailing list.

WORD PROCESSING BASICS

Scroll

If you create a long document, the computer screen cannot display all the text at the same time. You must scroll up or down to view and edit other parts of the document.

Word Wrap

A word processor automatically moves text you type to the next line. This is called word wrapping. When typing text, you only need to press Enter when you want to start a new paragraph.

When you use a word processor to type a letter, the text automatically wraps to the next line as you type.

Insertion Point

The flashing line on a screen is called the insertion point. It indicates where the text you type will appear in the document.

Select Text

Before performing certain tasks, you must select the text you want to work with. Selected text appears highlighted on the screen.

WORD PROCESSOR

Edit Text

After typing text in a document, you can easily add new text, delete text or move text to a new location. A word processor also remembers the last changes you made to a document and lets you undo, or cancel, the changes.

Thesaurus

A thesaurus helps you add variety to your writing. This feature lets you replace a word in a document with one that is more suitable.

Spelling and Grammar

A word processor includes a spell checker to find and correct spelling errors in a document. Some word processors will correct common spelling errors as you type.

Word processors also include a grammar checker to look for grammar, punctuation and stylistic errors.

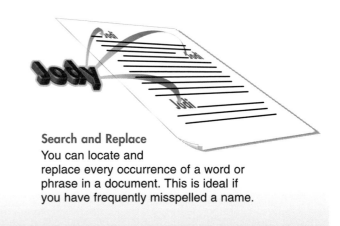

Search and Replace

You can locate and replace every occurrence of a word or phrase in a document. This is ideal if you have frequently misspelled a name.

FONT

A font refers to the design and size of characters in a document.

You will usually have all the fonts you need to create attractive documents. If you want more choices when creating documents, you can purchase additional fonts at most computer stores.

A font consists of three elements: typeface, type size and type style.

Arial
Brush Script MT
Bodoni
Courier New
Times New Roman

Typeface
Typeface refers to the design of characters.

10 point
12 point
14 point
18 point
24 point

Type Size
Type size refers to the size of characters and is measured in points. Most business documents use 10 or 12 point type. There are approximately 72 points in one inch.

Bold
Italic
SMALL CAPS
~~Strikethrough~~
Superscript[xxx]
Subscript[xxx]
<u>Underline</u>

Type Style
Type style refers to the appearance of characters.

WORD PROCESSOR

FORMAT A PARAGRAPH

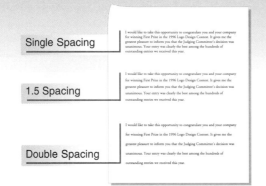

Line Spacing
You can make a document easier to read by changing the amount of space between the lines of text.

Tabs
You can use tabs to line up columns of information in a document. Use tabs instead of spaces to line up columns of text to ensure that a document will print correctly.

List
You can separate items in a list by beginning each item with a bullet or number. Bullets are useful for items in no particular order, such as a list of goals. Numbers are useful for items in a specific order, such as instructions for a recipe.

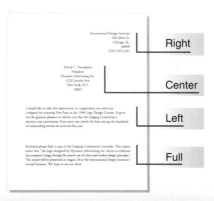

Text Alignment
You can enhance the appearance of a document by aligning paragraphs in different ways.

FORMAT A PAGE

Margin

A margin is the space between text and an edge of the paper. You can change the margin settings to adjust the length of a document or accommodate letterhead or other specialty paper.

Page Number

A word processor can number the pages in a document. You can specify the position and style of the page numbers.

Header and Footer

You can add a header or footer to each page of a document to display information such as the date or company name. A header appears at the top of each page. A footer appears at the bottom of each page.

Footnote and Endnote

Footnotes and endnotes provide additional information about text in a document. A footnote appears at the bottom of the page that contains the footnote number. An endnote appears at the end of the document.

SPREADSHEET

A spreadsheet program helps you manage personal and business finances.

Popular spreadsheet programs include Lotus 1-2-3 and Microsoft Excel.

SPREADSHEET APPLICATIONS

Manage Finances

You can use a spreadsheet program to perform calculations, analyze data and present information.

Manage Data in a List

A spreadsheet program lets you store a large collection of information such as a mailing or product list. Spreadsheet programs include tools for organizing, managing, sorting and retrieving data.

If you want greater control over a list stored on your computer, use a database program. Database programs are specifically designed to manage a list of data.

SPREADSHEET BASICS

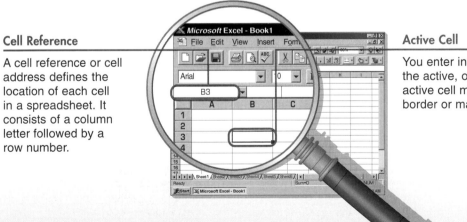

Column

A column is a vertical line of boxes. A letter identifies each column.

Row

A row is a horizontal line of boxes. A number identifies each row.

Cell

A cell is one box in a spreadsheet.

Cell Reference

A cell reference or cell address defines the location of each cell in a spreadsheet. It consists of a column letter followed by a row number.

Active Cell

You enter information into the active, or current, cell. The active cell may have a thick border or may appear shaded.

SPREADSHEET

A formula helps you calculate and analyze data in a spreadsheet.

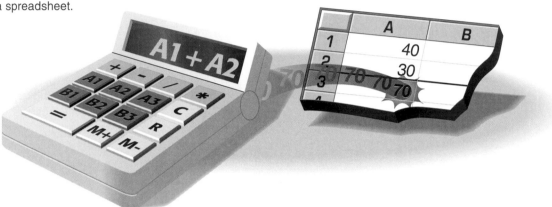

Spreadsheet programs perform calculations in the following order:

❶ Exponents (^)

❷ Multiply (*) and Divide (/)

❸ Add (+) and Subtract (−)

When entering formulas, use cell references (example: A1+A2) instead of actual data (example: 10+20) whenever possible.

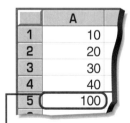

■ This cell contains the result of the formula:

=A1+A2+A3+A4

=10+20+30+40

=100

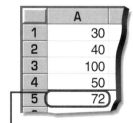

■ This cell contains the result of the formula:

=A1+A2+A3/A4

=30+40+100/50

=72

FORMULA TIPS

Automatic Recalculation

If you change a number used in a formula, you do not have to manually redo all the calculations. A spreadsheet program will automatically redo the calculation and display the new result.

This feature is very useful if you want to evaluate several possible scenarios, such as how different interest rates affect your mortgage payments. You can change one number and instantly see the effects on the rest of the data.

	A	B
1	Unit 1	30
2	Unit 2	80
3	**Total**	
4		

Using Parentheses

If you use parentheses ( ) in a formula, a spreadsheet program will calculate the data inside the parentheses first.

	A
1	10
2	70
3	50
4	20
5	220

■ This cell contains the result of the formula:

=A1*(A2-A3)+A4

=10*(70-50)+20

=220

Copy a Formula

After entering a formula in a spreadsheet, you can save time by copying the formula to other cells. A spreadsheet program will automatically change the cell references in the new formulas for you.

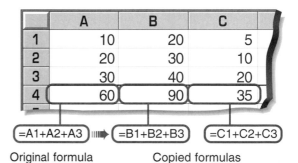

	A	B	C
1	10	20	5
2	20	30	10
3	30	40	20
4	60	90	35

| =A1+A2+A3 | ➡ | =B1+B2+B3 | =C1+C2+C3 |

Original formula   Copied formulas

SPREADSHEET

FUNCTION

A function is a ready-to-use formula that helps you perform specialized calculations.

The SUM function adds a list of numbers.

■ This cell contains the result of the function:

=SUM(A1:A4)

=A1+A2+A3+A4

=10+20+30+40

=100

The AVERAGE function calculates the average value of a list of numbers.

■ This cell contains the result of the function:

=AVERAGE(A1:A4)

=(A1+A2+A3+A4)/4

=(30+40+20+10)/4

=25

The MAX function finds the largest value in a list of numbers.

■ This cell contains the result of the function:

=MAX(A1:A4)

=70

EDIT A SPREADSHEET

Column Width and Row Height

You can change the width of columns and the height of rows to fit the data.

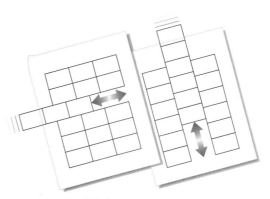

Edit Data

After entering data in a spreadsheet, you can add new data, delete data or move data to a new location. A spreadsheet program also remembers the last change you made and lets you undo, or cancel, the change.

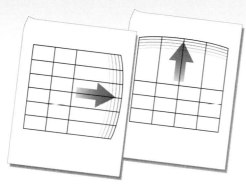

Complete a Series

A spreadsheet program can save you time by completing a series of numbers, text or time periods for you.

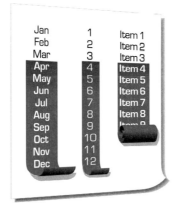

Rows and Columns

You can insert rows and columns to add new data. You can also delete rows and columns to remove data you do not need.

SPREADSHEET

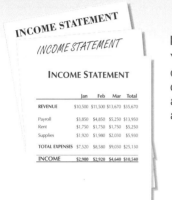

Font

You can change the design and size of characters to make a spreadsheet more appealing.

Number Appearance

You can change the look of numbers in a spreadsheet. A spreadsheet program offers many different ways to display numbers to make them easier to read and identify.

Borders, Shading and Color

You can add borders, shading and color to improve the appearance of a spreadsheet.

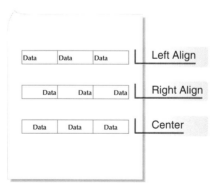

Data Alignment

You can change the position of data in each cell of a spreadsheet. For example, you can center all titles and right align all numbers.

CHART

A chart lets you graphically display
the data in a spreadsheet.

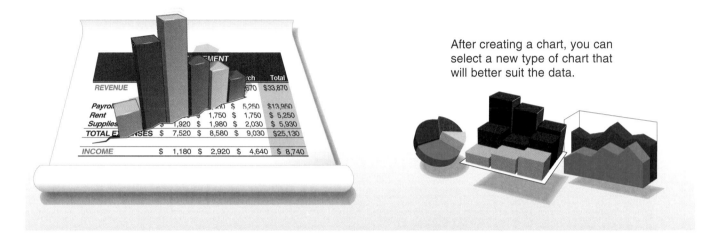

After creating a chart, you can
select a new type of chart that
will better suit the data.

Parts of a Chart

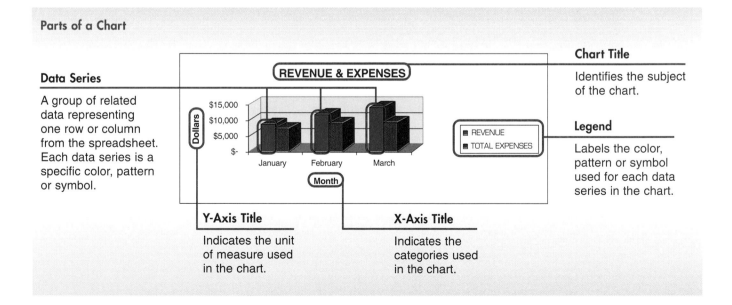

Data Series

A group of related
data representing
one row or column
from the spreadsheet.
Each data series is a
specific color, pattern
or symbol.

Chart Title

Identifies the subject
of the chart.

Legend

Labels the color,
pattern or symbol
used for each data
series in the chart.

Y-Axis Title

Indicates the unit
of measure used
in the chart.

X-Axis Title

Indicates the
categories used
in the chart.

DATABASE

A database program helps you manage large collections of information.

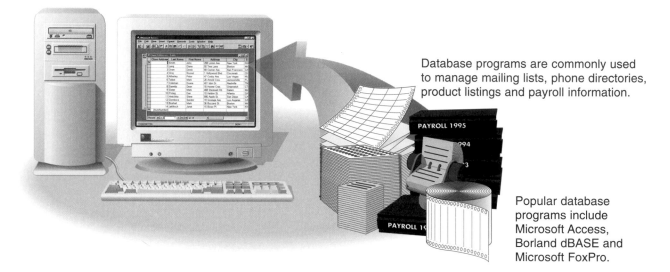

Database programs are commonly used to manage mailing lists, phone directories, product listings and payroll information.

Popular database programs include Microsoft Access, Borland dBASE and Microsoft FoxPro.

DATABASE APPLICATIONS

Store Data

You can use a database program to keep large collections of information organized and up-to-date.

Analyze Data

You can perform calculations on the information in a database. You can then analyze the results to make quick, accurate and informed decisions.

Create Reports

You can use the information in a database to create reports and presentations.

MANAGE INFORMATION

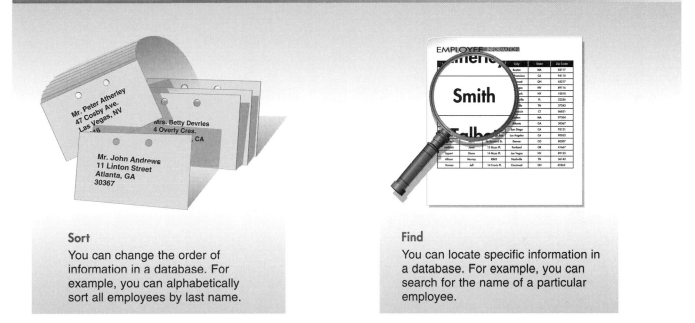

Sort

You can change the order of information in a database. For example, you can alphabetically sort all employees by last name.

Find

You can locate specific information in a database. For example, you can search for the name of a particular employee.

Query

You can create a query, which asks a database program to find information that meets certain criteria, or conditions. This lets you gather information of interest to you.

For example, a query can gather information on employees who sold more than 1000 units of product A last month. You can use the results of a query to create a report.

DATABASE

Table

A table is a collection of information about a specific topic, such as a mailing or product list. A database can consist of one or more tables.

Client Addresses : Table

Last Name	First Name	Address	City	State	Zip Code
Smith	John	258 Linton Ave.	New York	NY	10010-
Lang	Diane	50 Tree Lane	Boston	MA	02117-
Oram	Derek	68 Cacker Ave.	San Francisco	CA	94110-
Gray	Russel	1 Hollywood Blvd.	Cincinnati	OH	45217-
Atherley	Peter	47 Cosby Ave.	Las Vegas	NV	89116-
Talbot	Mark	26 Arnold Cres.	Jacksonville	FL	32256-
Coleman	Duane	401 Idon Dr.	Nashville	TN	37243-
Sanvido	Dean	16 Hoover Cres.	Greenwich	CT	06831-
Slater	Mark	468 Starewell Rd.	Salem	MA	97304-
Pozeg	Dan	10 Heldon St.	Atlanta	GA	30367-
Hretchka	Steve	890 Apple St.	San Diego	CA	92121-
Gombocz	Sandor	18 Goulage Ave.	Los Angeles	CA	90032-
Boshart	Mark	36 Buzzard St.	Boston	MA	02118-
Jaklitsch	Janet	15 Bizzo Pl.	New York	NY	10020-

Record: 1 of 14

Field Name

A field name identifies the information contained in a field.

Record

A record is a collection of information about one person, place or thing. For example, a record could contain the name and address of a client.

Field

A field is a single piece of information in a record. For example, a field could be the first name of a client.

You can use a form to help you enter data into a database. A form has boxes that clearly show you where to enter data.

Addresses

Address ID	1
First Name	John
Last Name	Smith
Address	258 Linton Ave.
City	New York
State/Province	NY
Postal Code	10010-
Country	US
Spouse Name	Kristin

Home Phone	(212) 555-1234
Work Phone	(212) 555-6789
Work Extension	507
Fax Number	(212) 555-6790

Preview Fact Sheet...   Dial...   Page: 1 2

Record: 1 of 1

TYPES OF DATABASES

EMPLOYEE PHONE NUMBERS

Name	Department	Phone Number
Allison, Steve	Accounting	555-1762
Atherly, Peter	Sales	555-2298
Boshart, Mark	Ordering	555-1270
Coleman, Dale	Sales	555-8851
Lang, Kristin	Shipping	555-9993
Lippert, Janet	Accounting	555-0042
Oram, Derek	Maintenance	555-7148
Sanvido, Dean	Service	555-0128
Smith, John	Sales	555-7018
Talbot, Mark	Ordering	555-1510

Flat File Database

A flat file database stores information in a single table.

A flat file database is easy to set up and learn. This type of database is ideal for simple lists, such as phone number and mailing lists.

Relational Database

A relational database lets you take information from different sources and organize the information in a single database.

CLIENT ADDRESSES

Name	Address	City	State
Atherly, Peter	15 River St.	La Jolia	CA
Coleman, Dale	82 15th Ave.	New York	NY
Lang, Kristin	24 Ladner Cr.	Cleveland	OH
Oram, Derek	7 Pindar Rd.	Seattle	WA
Sanvido, Dean	60 Norfolk St.	Salem	NH
Smith, John	31 6th Ave.	New York	NY
Talbot, Mark	116 West St.	Marietta	GA

ORDER INFORMATION

#	Product	Quantity	Name
1	C28505	30	Smith, John
2	C48851	100	Oram, Derek
3	C33709	300	Atherley, Peter
4	C40287	25	Smith, John
5	C58209	150	Coleman, Dale
6	C48851	20	Lang, Kristin
7	C33709	35	Sanvido, Dean

INVENTORY

Product	Price	In Stock
C20595	$80.00	12468
C28505	$20.00	1469
C29858	$30.00	50277
C33709	$45.00	6588
C40287	$19.99	206
C48851	$14.99	995
C58209	$79.00	50

A relational database stores information in two or more tables. Each table contains information on a different topic, such as client addresses, order information or inventory.

The tables in a relational database are related, or linked. If you change the information in one table, the same information will automatically change in all other tables. This makes updating fast and accurate.

A relational database is powerful and flexible, but difficult to set up and learn. This type of database is ideal for invoicing, accounting and inventory.

DESKTOP PUBLISHING

A desktop publishing (DTP) program helps you create professional documents by integrating text and graphics on a page.

You can use a desktop publishing program to create newsletters, brochures, manuals, flyers, advertisements, magazines and books.

Popular desktop publishing programs include Adobe PageMaker, Corel Ventura Publisher and QuarkXPress.

ADD TEXT AND GRAPHICS

Text

You can enter text directly into a desktop publishing document. You can also enter text into a word processor and then place the text in a desktop publishing document.

Graphics

You can create graphics using a separate program and then place the graphics in a desktop publishing document. You can only create very simple graphics with a desktop publishing program.

SERVICE BUREAU

A service bureau is a company that can produce high-quality printouts of your desktop publishing documents. Other services offered by service bureaus include slide preparation and high-quality scanning.

PAGE LAYOUT

Master Page
A master page contains elements that are repeated throughout a desktop publishing document, such as page numbers and headings.

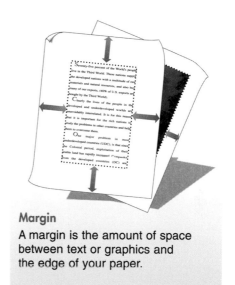

Margin
A margin is the amount of space between text or graphics and the edge of your paper.

Column Guides
Column guides are vertical lines that help you line up text and graphics on a page.

Paragraph Style
A paragraph style is a group of settings that you save and then apply to sections of text in a document.

Paragraph styles save you time and help give the document a consistent design.

DESKTOP PUBLISHING

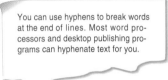

Word Wrap
A desktop publishing program lets you change the way text flows around a graphic.

Leading
You can change the spacing between lines of text.

Tracking
You can make text easier to read by changing the space between groups of characters.

Hyphenation
Hyphenation lets you break words at the end of lines in a desktop publishing document.

You can use hyphens to break words at the end of lines. Most word processors and desktop publishing programs can hyphenate text for you.

Font
You can use different character designs, sizes and styles in a document.

Serif Font
A serif font has short lines added to the top and bottom of each character.

Sans-Serif Font
A sans-serif font does not have short lines added to the top and bottom of each character.

WORK WITH GRAPHICS

A desktop publishing program gives you control over the graphics in a document.

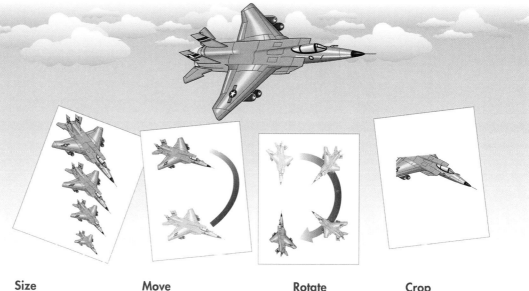

Size
Make a graphic larger or smaller.

Move
Change the position of a graphic on a page.

Rotate
Turn or spin a graphic.

Crop
Trim part of a graphic.

Clip Art
Clip art is a collection of ready-made graphics you can add to your documents. Some desktop publishing programs include a selection of clip art. You can also buy clip art at computer stores.

Scanned Images
You can use a scanner to copy images, such as photographs and drawings, into a desktop publishing document. A scanner is a device that reads text and images into a computer.

APPLICATION SUITE

An application suite is a collection of programs sold together in one package.

Cost
Buying programs as part of an application suite costs less than buying each program individually.

Easy To Use
Programs in an application suite share a common design and work in a similar way. Once you learn one program, you can easily learn the others.

Since all the programs in an application suite come from the same manufacturer, you may not get the best combination of features for your needs. Make sure you evaluate all the programs in an application suite before making your purchase.

APPLICATION SUITE PROGRAMS

Most application suites include four types of programs. Some application suites also offer additional programs, such as a scheduling program that lets you keep track of appointments.

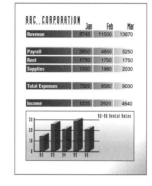

Word Processing Program

A word processing program lets you create documents, such as letters and reports.

Spreadsheet Program

A spreadsheet program lets you manage and analyze financial information.

Presentation Program

A presentation program lets you design presentations.

Database Program

A database program lets you manage large collections of information, such as a mailing list or payroll. The database program may only be included in higher-priced versions of the suite.

POPULAR APPLICATION SUITES

Microsoft Office is the most popular application suite.

Other application suites include Corel WordPerfect Suite and Lotus SmartSuite.

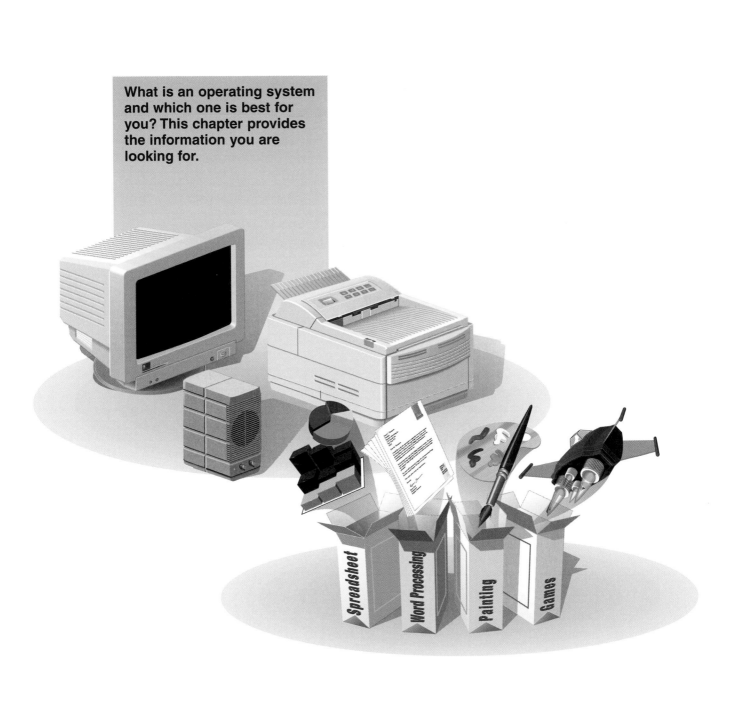

What is an operating system and which one is best for you? This chapter provides the information you are looking for.

Spreadsheet

Word Processing

Painting

Games

CHAPTER 7

OPERATING SYSTEMS

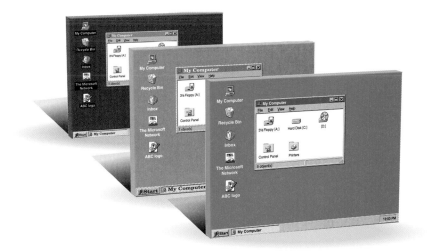

INTRODUCTION TO OPERATING SYSTEMS

An operating system is the software that controls the overall activity of a computer.

An operating system ensures that all parts of a computer system work together smoothly and efficiently.

OPERATING SYSTEM FUNCTIONS

Control Hardware

An operating system controls the different parts of a computer system and enables all the parts to work together.

Run Application Software

An operating system starts and runs application software, such as Microsoft Word and Lotus 1-2-3.

Manage Information

An operating system provides ways to manage and organize information stored on a computer. You can use an operating system to sort, copy, move, delete or view files.

POPULAR OPERATING SYSTEMS

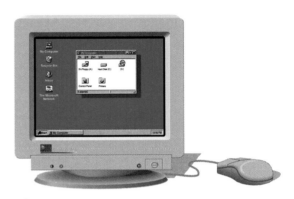

MS-DOS

MS-DOS stands for Microsoft Disk Operating System. MS-DOS displays lines of text on the screen. You perform tasks by typing short commands.

Windows

Windows displays a graphical screen. You use a mouse to perform tasks.

Windows is a Graphical User Interface (GUI, pronounced "gooey"). A GUI allows you to use pictures instead of words to perform tasks. This makes Windows easier to use than MS-DOS.

PLATFORM

A platform refers to the type of operating system used by a computer, such as MS-DOS or Windows. Programs used on one platform will usually not work on another platform. For example, you cannot use Word for Windows on a computer running only MS-DOS.

MS-DOS

MS-DOS is an operating system that performs tasks using text commands you enter.

MS-DOS stands for Microsoft Disk Operating System.

ENTER A COMMAND

Command Prompt

The command prompt (C:\>) tells you that MS-DOS is ready to accept a command.

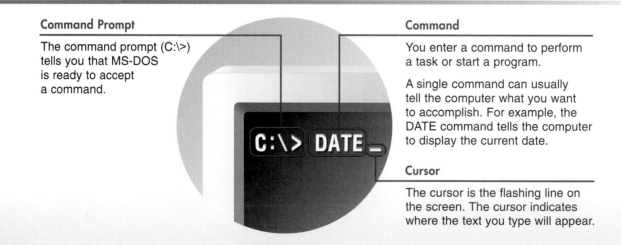

Command

You enter a command to perform a task or start a program.

A single command can usually tell the computer what you want to accomplish. For example, the DATE command tells the computer to display the current date.

Cursor

The cursor is the flashing line on the screen. The cursor indicates where the text you type will appear.

FILE ORGANIZATION

Like folders in a filing cabinet, MS-DOS uses directories to organize the data stored on a computer.

The root directory (C:\) is the main directory. All other directories are located within this directory.

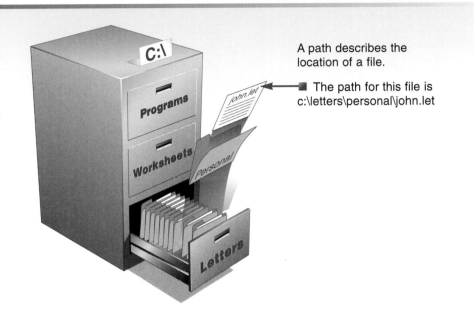

A path describes the location of a file.

■ The path for this file is c:\letters\personal\john.let

FILE NAME

When you store a file on a computer, you must give the file a name. An MS-DOS file name cannot contain any spaces. A file name consists of a name and an extension, separated by a period.

The name describes the contents of a file and can have up to eight characters.

The extension identifies the type of file and consists of three characters.

UTILITIES

MS-DOS 6.0 and later versions include special utilities to protect files and optimize a computer. For example, one program finds and repairs disk errors.

WINDOWS 3.1

Windows 3.1 works with MS-DOS to control the overall activity of a computer.

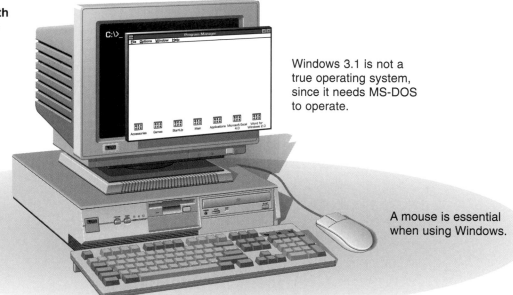

Windows 3.1 is not a true operating system, since it needs MS-DOS to operate.

A mouse is essential when using Windows.

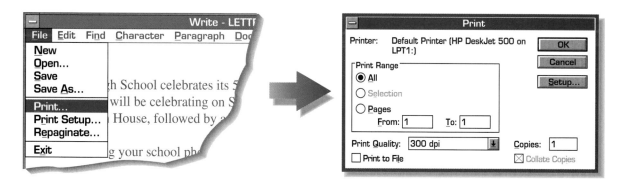

Menu

A menu lists related commands. You select a command from a menu to accomplish a task. For example, the **Print** command lets you produce a paper copy of a document.

Dialog Box

When you select a command, a dialog box may appear. A dialog box lets you select options before carrying out a command. For example, the Print dialog box lets you choose which pages you want to print.

THE WINDOWS 3.1 SCREEN

Windows 3.1 displays pictures on
the screen to help you perform tasks.
This makes Windows 3.1 easier to
use than MS-DOS.

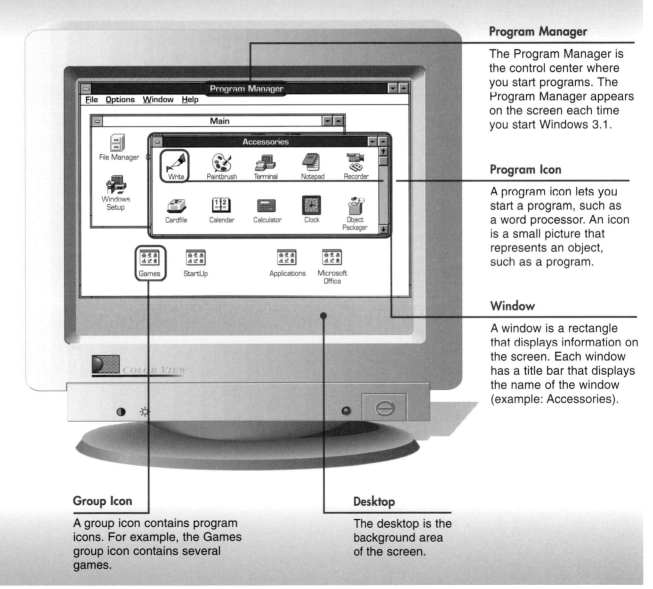

Program Manager

The Program Manager is
the control center where
you start programs. The
Program Manager appears
on the screen each time
you start Windows 3.1.

Program Icon

A program icon lets you
start a program, such as
a word processor. An icon
is a small picture that
represents an object,
such as a program.

Window

A window is a rectangle
that displays information on
the screen. Each window
has a title bar that displays
the name of the window
(example: Accessories).

Group Icon

A group icon contains program
icons. For example, the Games
group icon contains several
games.

Desktop

The desktop is the
background area
of the screen.

WINDOWS 3.1

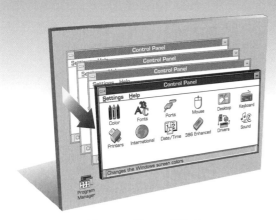

Move or Size a Window

You can move a window to a different location on a screen. You can also change the size of a window to display more of its contents.

Control Panel

The Control Panel lets you change the way Windows 3.1 looks and acts. For example, you can change the colors displayed on the screen.

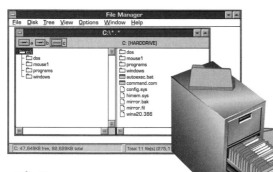

File Manager

The File Manager lets you view and organize all the files stored on a computer. Windows 3.1 uses directories to organize information, just as you would use folders to organize papers in a filing cabinet.

Accessories

Windows 3.1 provides several accessories, or mini-programs, that let you accomplish simple tasks, such as writing letters and drawing pictures.

WORK WITH MULTIPLE PROGRAMS

Windows 3.1 lets you run several programs at the same time and switch between the programs. For example, while writing a letter, you can switch to another program to check your sales figures.

You can easily exchange information between programs in Windows 3.1. For example, you can place a drawing in a letter.

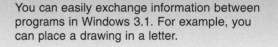

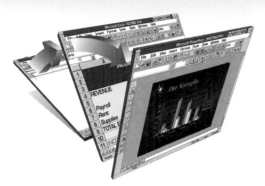

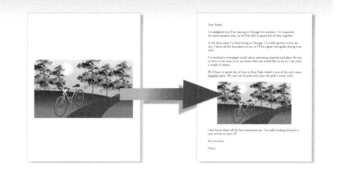

WINDOWS FOR WORKGROUPS 3.11

Windows for Workgroups (WfWG) 3.11 is a more powerful version of Windows 3.1. Like Windows 3.1, this program is not a true operating system, since it needs MS-DOS to operate.

Windows for Workgroups 3.11 lets you share files and printers with other computers connected to a network and includes programs for electronic mail and scheduling.

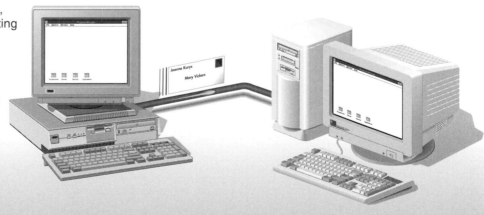

WINDOWS 95

Windows 95 is the successor of Windows 3.1. This operating system is more graphical and easier to use than Windows 3.1.

Windows 95 is a true operating system because it does not need MS-DOS to operate.

Window

A window is a rectangle that displays information on the screen. Each window has a title bar that displays the name of the window (example: My Computer).

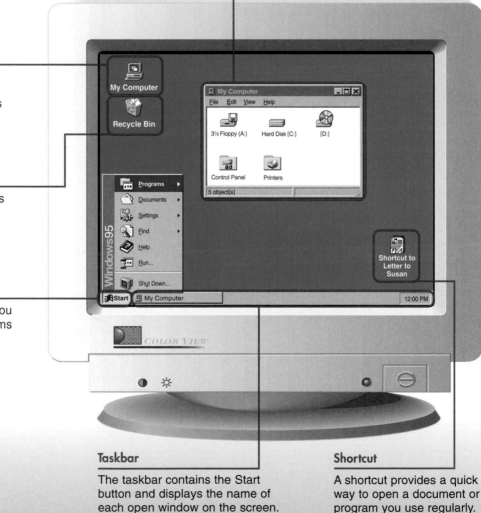

My Computer

My Computer lets you browse through all the folders and documents stored on a computer.

Recycle Bin

The Recycle Bin stores all the documents you delete and allows you to recover them later.

Start Button

The Start button lets you quickly access programs and documents.

Taskbar

The taskbar contains the Start button and displays the name of each open window on the screen.

Shortcut

A shortcut provides a quick way to open a document or program you use regularly.

WINDOWS 95 FEATURES

Customize Windows 95

You can easily change the way Windows 95 looks and acts. You can change the colors displayed on the screen or adjust the date and time set in the computer.

Document Names

You can use up to 255 characters, including spaces, to name a document in Windows 95. This lets you give your documents descriptive names so they are easy to identify.

Plug and Play

Windows 95 supports the Plug and Play technology. This technology lets you add new features to a computer without complex and time-consuming installation procedures.

Windows Explorer

Like a map, Windows Explorer shows you the location of each folder and document on a computer. You can use Windows Explorer to move, open, print or delete documents.

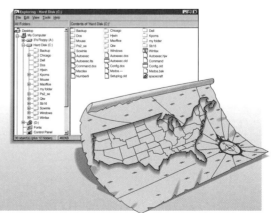

WINDOWS 95

WordPad and Paint

Windows 95 comes with a word processing program, called WordPad, that lets you create simple documents such as letters and memos. Windows 95 also includes a drawing program, called Paint, that lets you create pictures.

Computer Performance

Windows 95 comes with several features that will improve the performance of a computer. For example, the ScanDisk feature will search for and repair hard disk errors.

Backup

The Backup feature lets you copy important information stored on a computer to floppy disks or tape cartridges. This helps protect the information in case the original files are stolen or damaged due to viruses or computer failure.

Briefcase

The Briefcase feature lets you easily transfer files between your office and portable computers. This feature is useful if you work at home or while traveling. When you return to the office, Briefcase will update any documents you changed.

EXCHANGE INFORMATION

Microsoft Exchange

Windows 95 comes with Microsoft Exchange. This feature lets you exchange electronic mail with other people on a network or the Internet. You can also use this feature to send faxes to other computers or fax machines.

Networking

Windows 95 comes with features that let you share information and printers on a network. The Network Neighborhood feature lets you browse through and access information on all computers on a network. When at home or traveling, you can use the Dial-Up Networking feature to access information on the network at work.

WINDOWS NT

Windows NT is a powerful operating system that provides excellent security features. Like Windows 95, Windows NT is a true operating system and can use up to 255 characters to name documents. Windows NT was designed for users with powerful computer systems.

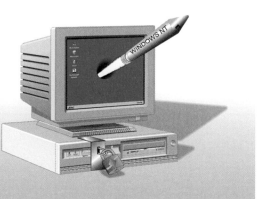

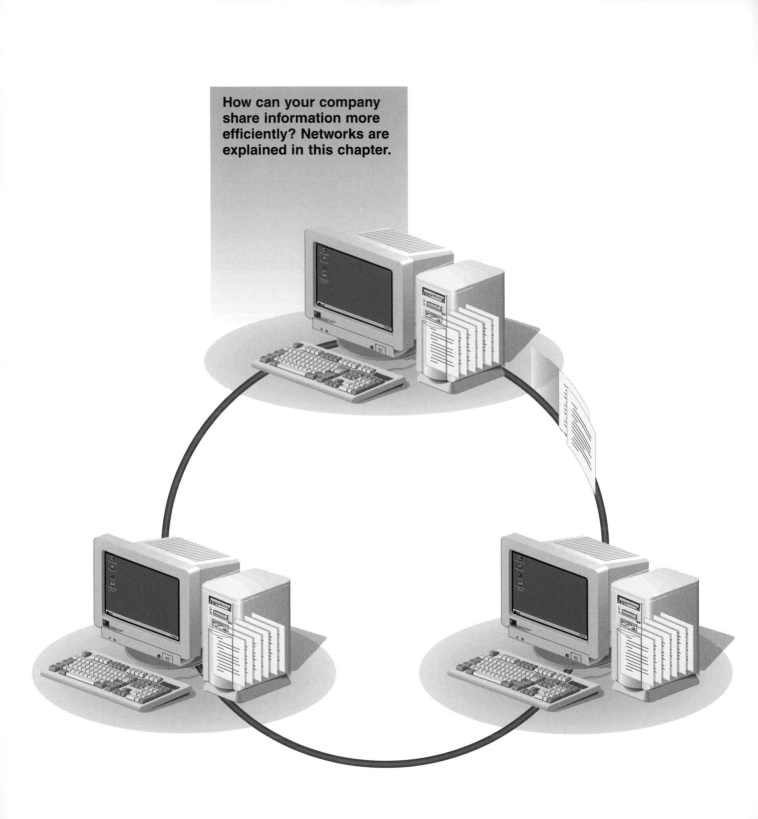

How can your company share information more efficiently? Networks are explained in this chapter.

NETWORKS

INTRODUCTION TO NETWORKS

A network is a group of connected computers that allow people to share information and equipment.

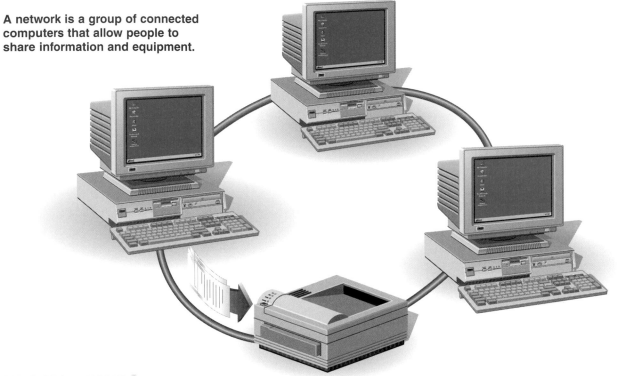

TYPES OF NETWORKS

Local Area Network

A Local Area Network (LAN) is a network that connects computers within a small geographic area, such as a building.

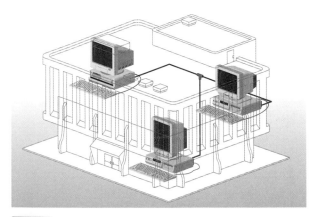

Wide Area Network

A Wide Area Network (WAN) is a network that connects computers across a large geographic area, such as a city or country. A WAN can transmit information by telephone line, microwave or satellite.

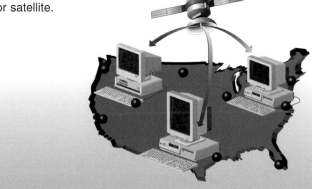

NETWORK ADVANTAGES

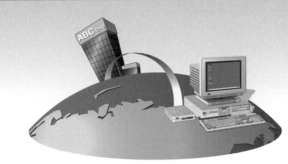

Work Away From Office

When traveling or at home, you can connect to the network at work to exchange messages and files.

Eliminate Sneakernet

Sneakernet refers to physically carrying information from one computer to another to exchange information. A computer network eliminates the need for sneakernet.

Share Information

Networks let you easily share data and programs. You can exchange documents, electronic mail, video, sound and images.

Share Equipment

Computers connected to a network can share equipment, such as a printer or modem.

NETWORK ADMINISTRATOR

A network administrator manages the network and makes sure the network runs smoothly. A network administrator may also be called a network manager, information systems manager or system administrator.

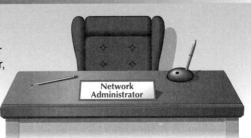

NETWORK APPLICATIONS

Electronic Mail

You can exchange electronic mail (e-mail) with other people on a network. Electronic mail saves paper and provides a fast and convenient way to exchange ideas and request information.

Groupware

Groupware is software that helps people on a network coordinate and manage projects. Groupware packages usually let you exchange electronic mail, schedule meetings, participate in online discussions and share corporate information. Popular groupware packages include Lotus Notes and Novell GroupWise.

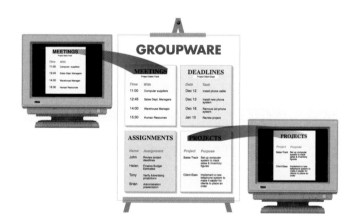

Videoconferencing

Videoconferencing lets you have face-to-face conversations with other people on a network, whether they are around the corner or on the other side of the country. Using videoconferencing software and equipment, you can see and hear the people you are communicating with.

PARTS OF A NETWORK

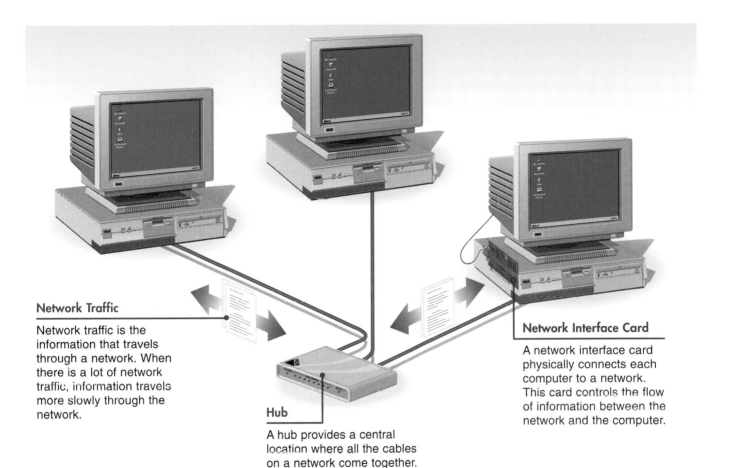

Network Traffic

Network traffic is the information that travels through a network. When there is a lot of network traffic, information travels more slowly through the network.

Hub

A hub provides a central location where all the cables on a network come together.

Network Interface Card

A network interface card physically connects each computer to a network. This card controls the flow of information between the network and the computer.

Cables

Cables connect computers and equipment to a network. There are four main types of cables—coaxial, Unshielded Twisted Pair (UTP), Shielded Twisted Pair (STP) and fiber optic. Fiber optic cable is the most expensive type of cable, but it can carry information faster and over longer distances.

HOW INFORMATION IS STORED

PEER-TO-PEER NETWORK

All the people on a peer-to-peer network store their files on their own computers. Anyone on the network can access files stored on any other computer.

A peer-to-peer network provides a simple and inexpensive way to connect fewer than ten computers.

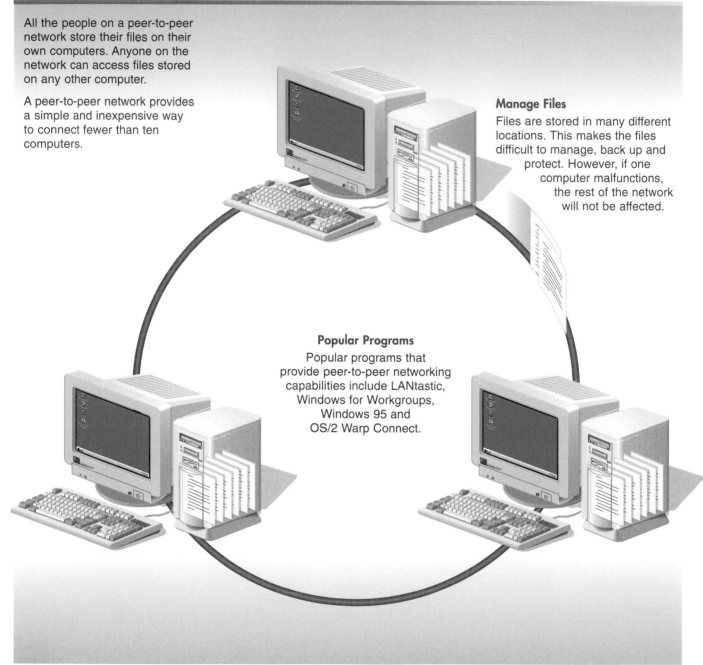

Manage Files

Files are stored in many different locations. This makes the files difficult to manage, back up and protect. However, if one computer malfunctions, the rest of the network will not be affected.

Popular Programs

Popular programs that provide peer-to-peer networking capabilities include LANtastic, Windows for Workgroups, Windows 95 and OS/2 Warp Connect.

CLIENT/SERVER NETWORK

All the people on a client/server network store their files on a central computer. Everyone connected to the network can access the files stored on the central computer.

A client/server network provides a highly efficient way to connect ten or more computers or computers exchanging large amounts of information.

Server
The server is the central computer that stores the files of every person on the network.

Manage Files
All the files are stored on the server. This makes the files easy to manage, back up and protect. However, if the server malfunctions, the entire network will be affected.

Popular Programs
Popular programs that provide client/server networking capabilities include NetWare and Windows NT.

Client
A client is a computer that can access information stored on the server.

HOW INFORMATION IS EXCHANGED

ETHERNET

Ethernet is the most popular and least expensive way information can travel through a network. Ethernet is the easiest type of network to set up.

Speed

Ethernet can send information through a network at a speed of 10 megabits per second (Mb/s). Fast Ethernet can send information through a network at a speed of 100 megabits per second (Mb/s).

How Ethernet Works

Ethernet works the same way people talk during a polite conversation. Each computer waits for a pause before sending information through a network.

When two computers try to send information at the same time, a collision occurs. After a moment, the computers resend the information.

TOKEN-RING

Token-ring is an older type of network often found in large organizations, such as banks and insurance companies.

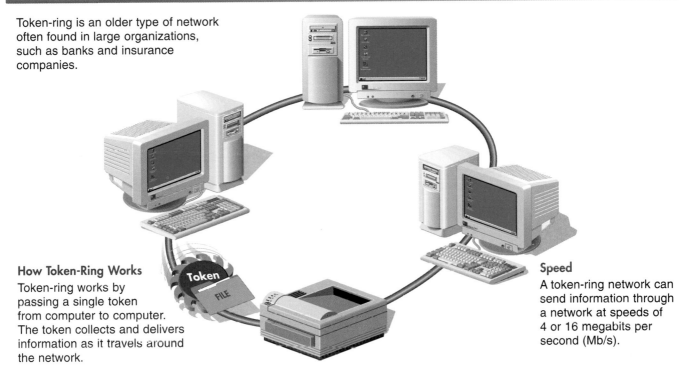

How Token-Ring Works

Token-ring works by passing a single token from computer to computer. The token collects and delivers information as it travels around the network.

Speed

A token-ring network can send information through a network at speeds of 4 or 16 megabits per second (Mb/s).

ATM

Asynchronous Transfer Mode (ATM) is a newer, more powerful and more expensive way to exchange information on a network. Today, companies often use ATM to transfer information between two separate networks.

As the cost of ATM lowers, ATM will be used more frequently to transfer information between individual computers within a network.

How ATM Works

ATM works by sending information through a network in equal-sized pieces, called fixed packets.

Speed

ATM can send information through a network at speeds of 25, 155 or 622 megabits per second (Mb/s).

NETWORK SECURITY

FIREWALL

A firewall is special software or hardware designed to protect a private computer network from unauthorized access. Firewalls are used by corporations, banks and research facilities to keep information private and secure.

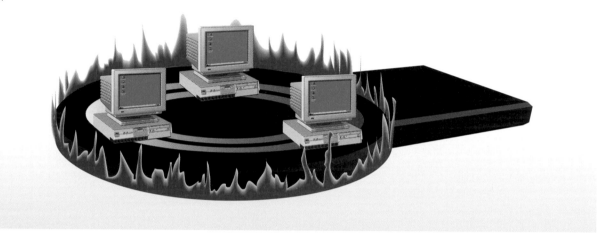

USER NAME AND PASSWORD

You usually have to enter a user name and password when you want to access information on a network. This ensures that only authorized people can use the information stored on the network.

Choose a Password

When choosing a password, do not use words that people can easily associate with you, such as your name or favorite sport. The most effective password connects two words or number sequences with a special character (example: easy@123). To increase security, memorize your password and do not write it down.

happy#44
jim#96
easy@123

SECRET

INTRANET

An intranet is a small version of the Internet inside a corporate office.

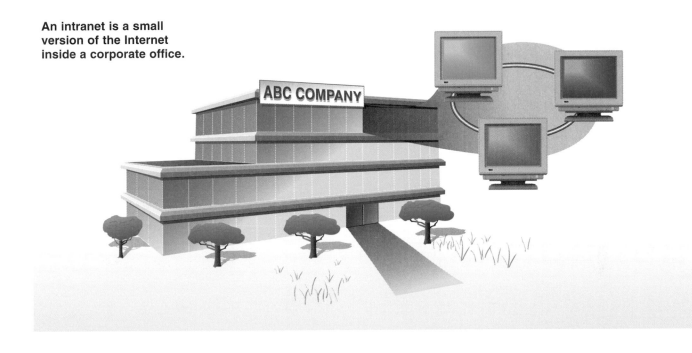

Information

An intranet is a very efficient and inexpensive way to make internal company documents available to employees. Companies use intranets to distribute information such as phone directories, product listings and job openings.

Programs

The program you use to browse through information on an intranet is the same program you would use to browse through information on the Web.

Connected Documents

Documents on an intranet are connected. Employees can select highlighted text in one document to display another, related document.

What is the Internet and how can I get connected? This chapter provides you with all the information you need to start exploring the Internet.

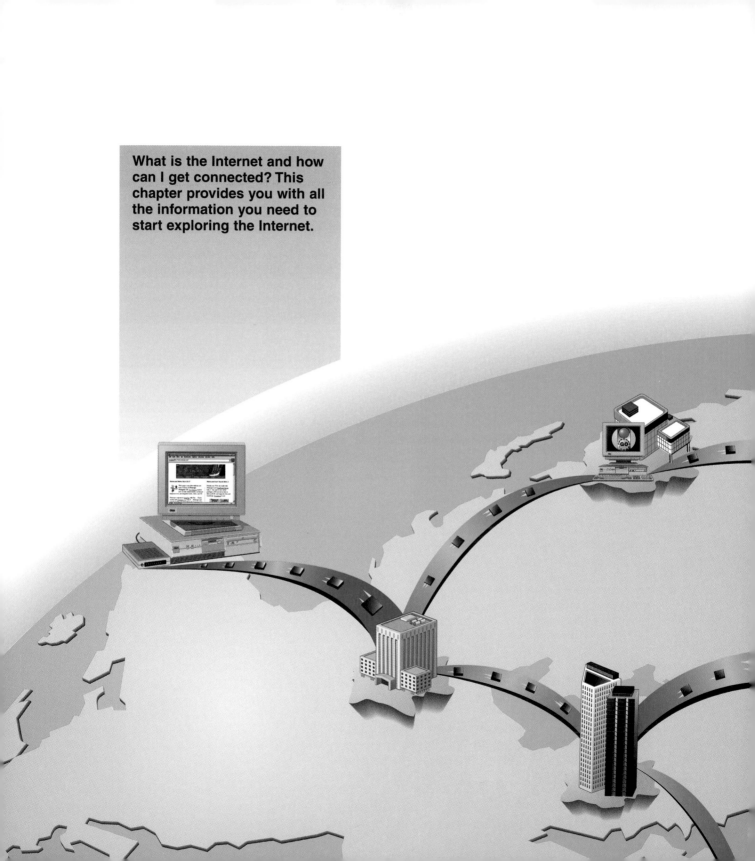

THE INTERNET

INTRODUCTION TO THE INTERNET

The Internet is the largest computer system in the world.

The Internet is often called the Net, the Information Superhighway or Cyberspace.

In the late 1960s, the U.S. Defense department began the Internet as a military research project. The network quickly grew to include scientists and researchers across the United States. Eventually, schools, businesses and libraries around the world were on the Internet.

The Internet consists of thousands of connected networks around the world. A network is a collection of computers that are connected to share information.

Each government, company and organization is responsible for maintaining its own network.

If part of the Internet fails, information finds a new route around the disabled computers.

FREE INFORMATION

Most of the information on the Internet is free. Governments, universities, colleges, companies and individuals around the world provide free information to educate and entertain the public.

WHAT THE INTERNET OFFERS

ELECTRONIC MAIL

Exchanging electronic mail is the most popular feature on the Internet. You can exchange electronic mail with people around the world, including friends, colleagues, family members, customers and even people you meet on the Internet. Electronic mail is fast, easy, inexpensive and saves paper.

INFORMATION

The Internet gives you access to information on any subject imaginable. You can review newspapers, magazines, academic papers, government documents, television show transcripts, famous speeches, recipes, job listings, works by Shakespeare, airline schedules and much more. Governments, colleges, universities, companies and individuals all offer free information on the Internet.

PROGRAMS

Thousands of programs are available on the Internet. These programs include word processors, spreadsheets, games and much more.

ENTERTAINMENT

Hundreds of simple games are available for free on the Internet, including backgammon, chess, poker, football and much more.

The Internet also lets you review current movies, hear television theme songs, read movie scripts and have interactive conversations with people around the world—even celebrities.

DISCUSSION GROUPS

You can join discussion groups on the Internet to meet people around the world with similar interests. You can ask questions, discuss problems and read interesting stories.

There are thousands of discussion groups on topics such as the environment, food, humor, music, pets, photography, politics, religion, sports and television.

ONLINE SHOPPING

You can order goods and services on the Internet without ever leaving your desk. You can buy items such as books, computer programs, flowers, music CDs, pizza, stocks, used cars and much more.

HOW INFORMATION TRANSFERS

All computers on the Internet work together to transfer information back and forth around the world.

Packets

When you send information through the Internet, the information is broken down into smaller pieces, called packets. Each packet travels independently through the Internet and may take a different path to arrive at the intended destination.

When information arrives at its destination, the packets are reassembled.

TCP/IP

Transmission Control Protocol/Internet Protocol (TCP/IP) is a language computers on the Internet use to communicate with each other. TCP/IP divides information you send into packets and sends the packets across the Internet. When information arrives at the intended destination, TCP/IP ensures that all the packets arrived safely.

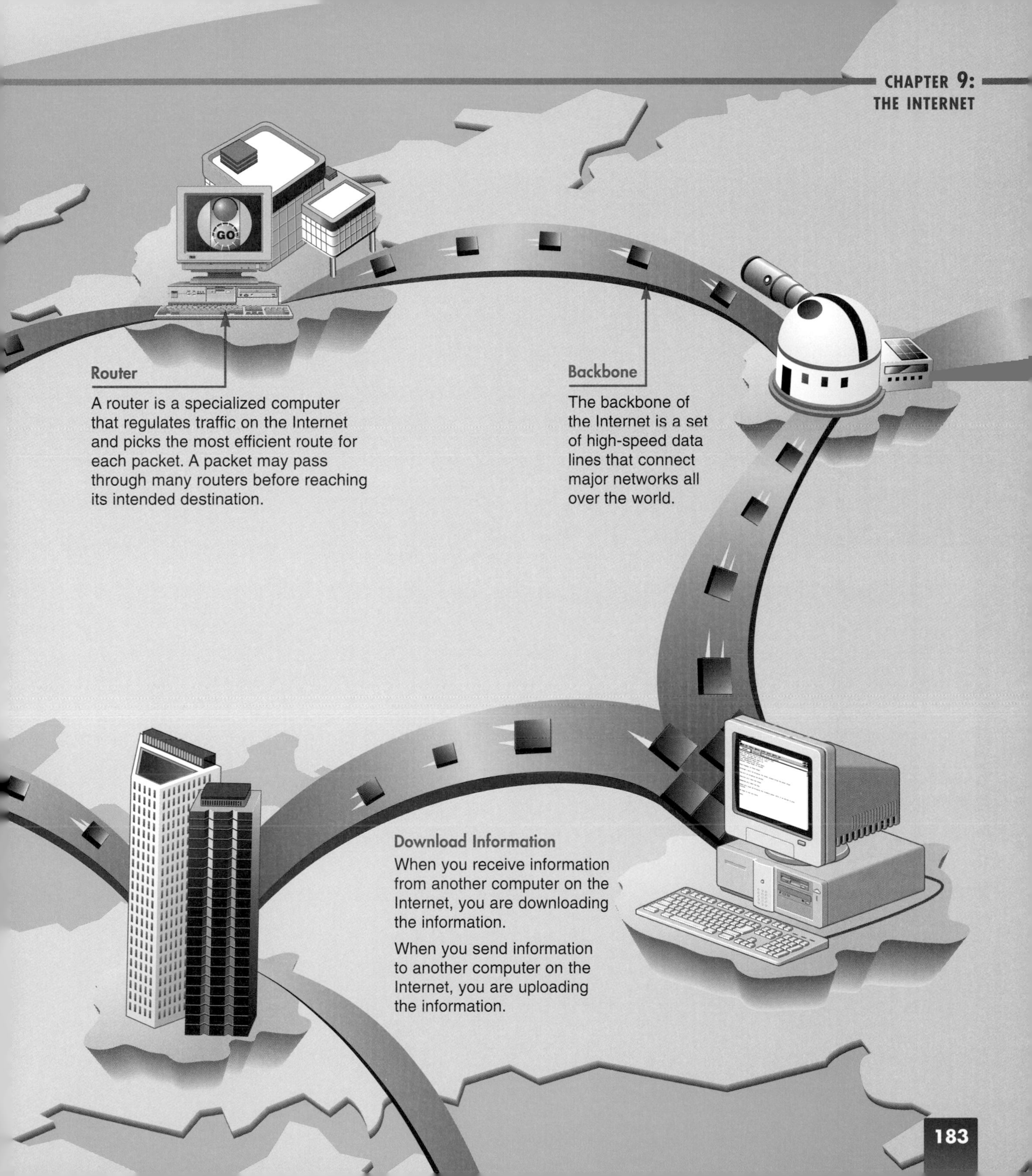

Router

A router is a specialized computer that regulates traffic on the Internet and picks the most efficient route for each packet. A packet may pass through many routers before reaching its intended destination.

Backbone

The backbone of the Internet is a set of high-speed data lines that connect major networks all over the world.

Download Information

When you receive information from another computer on the Internet, you are downloading the information.

When you send information to another computer on the Internet, you are uploading the information.

183

GETTING CONNECTED

You need specific equipment and programs to connect to the Internet.

COMPUTER

You can use any type of computer, such as an IBM-compatible or Macintosh computer, to connect to the Internet.

PROGRAMS

You need special programs to use the Internet. Most companies that connect you to the Internet provide the programs you need free of charge.

MODEM

You need a modem to connect to the Internet. Choose a modem with a speed of at least 14,400 bps, although a modem with a speed of 28,800 bps is recommended. For more information on modems, refer to page 54.

WAYS TO CONNECT

Connection Service

An Internet service provider (ISP) or commercial online service can connect you to the Internet for a fee.

Make sure you choose a connection service with a local telephone number to avoid long-distance charges.

Freenets

A freenet is a free, local service that provides community information and access to the Internet. Most freenets do not let you see graphics, so you can only view text on your screen.

Freenets can be difficult to connect to because they are often busy.

USER NAME AND PASSWORD

You have to enter a user name and password when you want to connect to the Internet. This ensures that you are the only one who can access your Internet account.

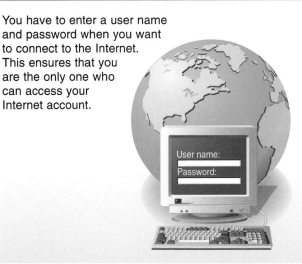

Choosing a Password

When choosing a password, do not use words that people can easily associate with you, such as your name or favorite sport. The most effective password connects two words or number sequences with a special character (example: blue@123). You should never write down your password in case someone else sees the password.

happy#44
jim#96
blue@123

GETTING CONNECTED

INTERNET SERVICE PROVIDER

An Internet Service Provider (ISP) is a company that gives you access to the Internet for a fee.

Cost

There are different ways an Internet service provider can charge you for the time you spend on the Internet. Many providers offer you a certain number of hours per day or month for a set fee. If you exceed the total number of hours, you are usually charged for every extra hour.

Some providers offer unlimited access to the Internet for a flat fee. Make sure you are aware of any hidden charges or restrictions.

Some providers charge a fee for setting up your connection to the Internet.

Busy Signals

Ask the provider how many members there are for each phone line. More than ten members for each phone line means you may get a busy signal when you try to connect.

INTERNET SERVICE PROVIDER FEATURES

Getting Help

Setting up a connection to an Internet service provider can be difficult. Find out if the provider offers customer support in the evenings and on weekends as well as during business hours.

Publish Web Pages

You can create Web pages to share business or personal information with people around the world. Look for a provider that will publish Web pages you create. Many providers let you publish and maintain Web pages for free.

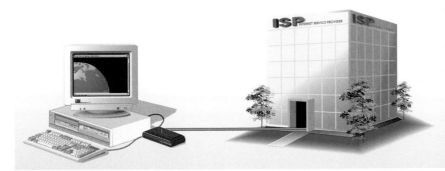

Type of Connection

There are three ways you can connect to an Internet service provider.

A Point-to-Point Protocol (PPP) connection is the most popular and most reliable way to connect to a provider using a modem. Serial Line Internet Protocol (SLIP) and Compressed SLIP (CSLIP) are older and less reliable ways to connect to a provider.

GETTING CONNECTED

COMMERCIAL ONLINE SERVICE

A commercial online service is a company that offers a vast amount of information and access to the Internet for a fee.

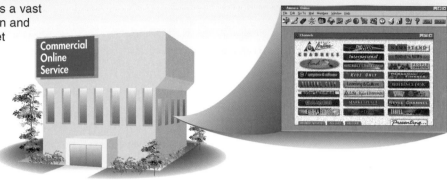

Cost

Most commercial online services let you try their service free of charge for a limited time. After the trial period, most online services offer a certain number of hours per day or month for a set fee.

If you exceed the total number of hours, you are usually charged for every extra hour you use the online service.

Most online services do not charge a fee for setting up your connection to the Internet.

POPULAR COMMERCIAL ONLINE SERVICES

Popular online services include America Online, CompuServe and The Microsoft Network.

America Online   **CompuServe**   **The Microsoft Network**

COMMERCIAL ONLINE SERVICE FEATURES

Information

An online service offers information such as daily news, stock quotes, weather reports, encyclopedias, dictionaries and magazines. This information is well-organized and easy to find, unlike information on the Internet.

Internet Access

All the major online services offer access to the Internet.

Getting Help

Setting up a connection to an online service is relatively easy. Online services usually provide good customer support for questions you may have.

Chat

Chatting is a very popular feature on online services. You can instantly communicate with other people connected to the service by simply typing back and forth. Chatting is a great way to meet people and exchange ideas.

When you chat, the text you type immediately appears on the screen of each person involved in the conversation.

Don't get tangled in the Web! After you read this chapter's discussion of Web browsers, shopping on the Web, multimedia and more, you might want to try creating a Web page of your own.

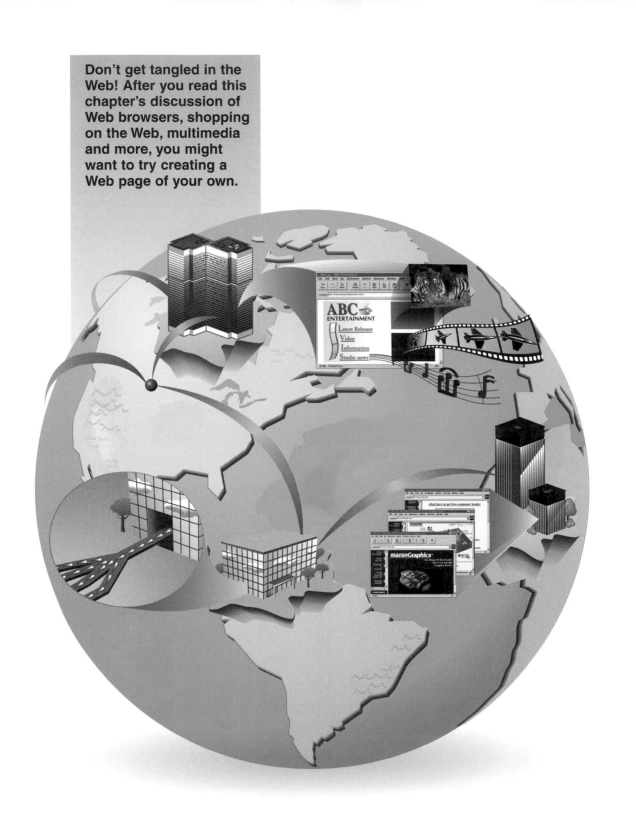

THE WORLD WIDE WEB

INTRODUCTION TO THE WEB

The World Wide Web is part of the Internet. The Web consists of a huge collection of documents stored on computers around the world.

The World Wide Web is also called the Web, WWW and W3.

Web Page

A Web page is a document on the Web. Web pages can include text, pictures, sound and video.

Avoid Traffic Jams

Each Web site can only let a certain number of people connect at once. If you are unable to connect to a site, try connecting at another time. The best time to connect is at night or on the weekend when fewer people are using the Internet.

Web Site

A Web site is a collection of Web pages maintained by a college, university, government agency, company or individual.

URL

Each Web page has a unique address, called the Uniform Resource Locator (URL). You can instantly display any Web page if you know its URL.

 All Web page URLs start with http (HyperText Transfer Protocol).

HYPERTEXT

Web pages are hypertext documents. A hypertext document contains highlighted text that connects to other pages on the Web. You can easily jump from one Web page to another by selecting the highlighted text.

Selecting highlighted text can take you to a page located on the same computer or a computer across the city, country or world.

WEB BROWSER

A Web browser is a program that lets you view and explore information on the Web.

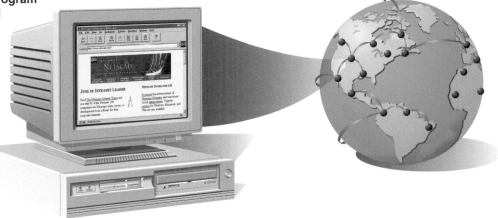

POPULAR BROWSERS

Netscape Navigator is currently the most popular browser. Other popular browsers include Microsoft Internet Explorer and NCSA Mosaic.

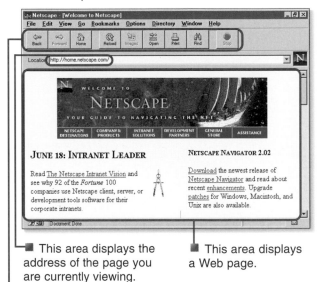

■ This area displays the address of the page you are currently viewing.

■ This area displays a Web page.

■ This area displays a toolbar to help you quickly perform common tasks.

HOME PAGE

The home page is the page that appears each time you start a Web browser.

You can choose any page on the Web as your home page. Make sure you choose a home page that provides a good starting point for exploring the Web.

WEB BROWSER FEATURES

Bookmarks

The bookmarks feature lets you store the addresses of Web pages you frequently visit. Bookmarks save you from having to remember and constantly retype your favorite Web page addresses. The bookmarks feature is also called a hotlist or favorites feature.

History

The History feature keeps track of all the pages you have viewed since you last started the Web browser. This feature lets you instantly return to any of the pages you have viewed.

Turn Off Graphics

Graphics may take a while to appear on the screen. You can save time by turning off the display of graphics. When you turn off the display of graphics, an icon (example:) will appear in place of any graphics.

GRAPHICS ON

GRAPHICS OFF

SHOPPING ON THE WEB

You can buy products and services on the Web without ever leaving your desk.

There are thousands of products you can buy on the Web, such as clothing, flowers, office supplies and computer programs.

The Web also offers a range of services, such as banking and financial or real estate advice.

COMPANIES

Thousands of companies have Web sites where you can get product information and buy products and services online.

You can view a list of companies on the Web at the following site:

http://www.directory.net

SHOPPING MALLS

There are shopping malls on the Web where you can view and buy products and services offered by many different companies.

You can view a list of shopping malls on the Web at the following site:

http://nsns.com/MouseTracks/HallofMalls.html

SECURITY ON THE WEB

Security is very important when you want to send confidential information such as credit card numbers or bank records over the Internet.

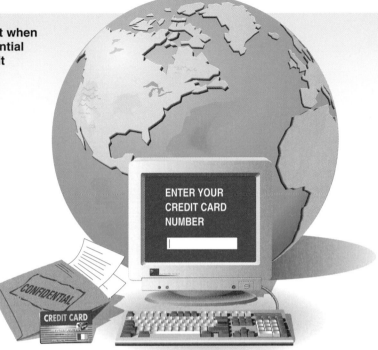

SECURE SITES

You can safely transfer confidential information to a secure site on the Web. The address of a secure site usually starts with https rather than http.

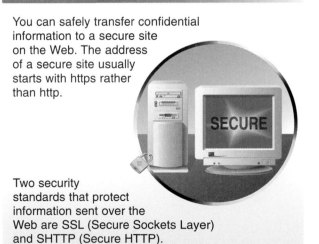

Two security standards that protect information sent over the Web are SSL (Secure Sockets Layer) and SHTTP (Secure HTTP).

RECOGNIZING SECURE SITES

Web browsers usually indicate if a site displayed on the screen is secure.

Netscape displays a broken key icon at the bottom of the screen when you are not at a secure site.

Netscape displays a solid key icon at the bottom of the screen when you are at a secure site.

WEB PAGE FEATURES

FRAMES

Some Web pages divide information into rectangular frames. Each frame can display a different document and has its own unique address.

FORMS

Some Web pages include forms that let you enter data. The information you type into a form travels across the Web to the computer that maintains the page.

Shopping sites often have forms that let you fill in your name, address and phone number to order products.

Search sites also have forms that let you enter the topic you want to search for.

TABLES

Some Web pages display information in tables. A table organizes information into an easy-to-follow, attractive format. Tables can include graphics as well as text.

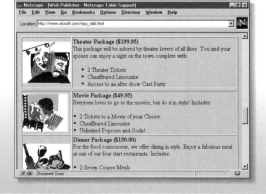

JAVA

Java is a programming language that allows Web pages to display animation and moving text, play music and much more.

Programs written in Java are called Java applets.

You can find many examples of Java at the following Web page:

http://www.gamelan.com

ANIMATED CHARACTERS

Java lets you watch animated characters move on a Web page.

MOVING TEXT

Java lets you view text that blinks or scrolls across the screen. Information such as stock quotes and weather reports can update before your eyes.

INTERACTION

Java lets you interact with information on the screen. You can play games, such as crossword puzzles and tic-tac-toe. You can also type in data and have a Java applet perform calculations, such as working out mortgage or car payments.

MULTIMEDIA ON THE WEB

A Web page can contain text, graphics, sound, video and animation.

A Web browser needs special programs, called plug-ins or helpers, to work with certain types of files on the Web. These programs perform tasks that a browser cannot perform on its own. Most plug-ins and helpers are available for free on the Web.

TRANSFER TIME

Some files take a while to transfer to your computer. A Web page usually shows you the size of a file to give you an indication of how long the file will take to transfer.

	File Size		Time
Bytes	Kilobytes (KB)	Megabytes (MB)	(estimated)
10,000,000	10,000	10	1 hour
5,000,000	5,000	5	30 minutes
2,500,000	2,500	2.5	15 minutes

Use this chart as a guide to determine how long a file will take to transfer to your computer.

This chart is based on transferring files with a 28,800 bps modem. A modem with a speed of 14,400 bps or lower will transfer files more slowly than shown in the chart.

GRAPHICS

You can view graphics such as album covers, pictures of celebrities and famous paintings on the Web.

Popular Files

There are common types of graphics files you will find on the Web.

Graphics Interchange Format (.gif)
Joint Photographics Expert Group (.jpeg or .jpg)

Inline Graphics

Most graphics on the Web are inline graphics. Inline graphics can include pictures, photographs, arrows and buttons.

Thumbnail Graphics

A thumbnail graphic is a small version of a larger graphic that transfers quickly to your computer. If you want to see the larger graphic, select the thumbnail graphic.

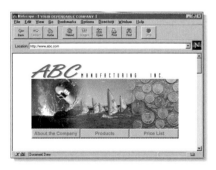

Imagemaps

An imagemap is a graphic divided into sections, called hotspots. Each hotspot contains a link to another page on the Web. Selecting a hotspot will take you to the linked page.

MULTIMEDIA ON THE WEB

You can view documents on the Web such as newspapers, magazines, plays, famous speeches and television show transcripts.

Text transfers quickly to your computer so you do not have to wait long to read text on a Web page.

Popular Files

There are common types of text files you will find on the Web.

Document (.doc)
HyperText Markup Language (.html or .htm)
Text (.txt)

SOUND

You can hear sound on the Web such as TV theme songs, movie soundtracks, sound effects and historical speeches.

You need a sound card and speakers to hear sound generated by a computer. A sound card is a device you place inside a computer to play high-quality sound.

Popular Files

There are common types of sound files you will find on the Web.

Audio Player (.au)
RealAudio (.ra or .ram)
Wave (.wav)

VIDEO AND ANIMATION

You can view video and animation on the Web such as movie clips, cartoons and interviews with celebrities.

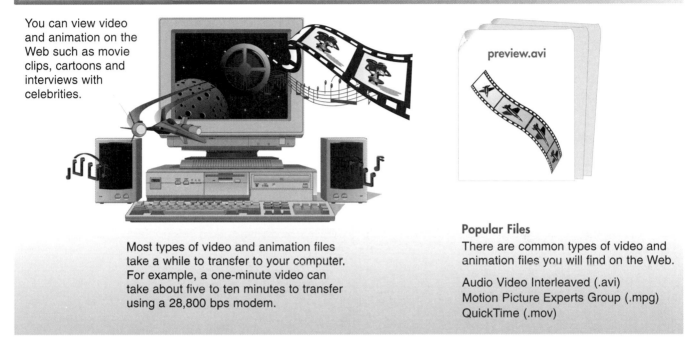

Most types of video and animation files take a while to transfer to your computer. For example, a one-minute video can take about five to ten minutes to transfer using a 28,800 bps modem.

preview.avi

Popular Files

There are common types of video and animation files you will find on the Web.

Audio Video Interleaved (.avi)
Motion Picture Experts Group (.mpg)
QuickTime (.mov)

3-D WORLDS

You can view three-dimensional worlds and objects on the Web.

3-D worlds are created using a language called Virtual Reality Modeling Language (VRML).

You can use your mouse or keyboard to move through three-dimensional rooms or walk around a virtual object.

SEARCH THE WEB

There are many free services you can use to find information on the Web. These services are called search tools.

A search tool catalogs Web pages to make them easier to find. Some search tools record every word on a Web page, while others only record the name of each page.

You can see a list of various search tools at the following Web sites:

http://www.search.com/alpha.html

http://home.netscape.com/home/internet-search.html

HOW SEARCH TOOLS FIND WEB PAGES

There are two ways a search tool finds pages on the Web.

Since hundreds of new pages are created each day, it is impossible for a search tool to catalog every new page on the Web.

Spiders

Most search tools have automated robots, called spiders, that travel around the Web looking for new pages.

Submissions

People submit information about pages they have created.

SEARCH METHODS

There are two ways a search tool can help you find information on the Web.

Search by Category

You can browse through categories such as arts, science and sports to find information that interests you.

Select a category of interest and a list of subcategories appears.

Continue to select subcategories until you find a page that interests you.

Search by Topic

You can search for a specific topic that interests you.

Type in a topic of interest.

When the search is complete, a list of pages containing the topic you specified appears.

SEARCH THE WEB

Alta Vista

Alta Vista lets you search for a specific topic of interest. You can choose to search Web pages or Usenet, a part of the Internet that contains discussion groups, called newsgroups.

You can access Alta Vista at the following Web site:

http://altavista.digital.com

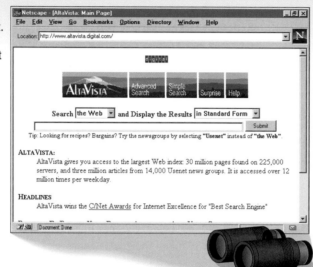

Alta Vista has a **Surprise** feature that takes you to randomly selected Web pages. This is a fun way to view pages on the Web.

Infoseek

Infoseek lets you search for a specific topic of interest or browse through categories, such as education or travel.

You can choose to search Web pages, e-mail addresses or Usenet, a part of the Internet that contains discussion groups, called newsgroups.

You can access Infoseek at the following Web site:

http://www.infoseek.com

Infoseek has a **Fast Facts** feature that gives you quick access to stock quotes and information about thousands of U.S. companies.

Lycos

Lycos lets you search for a specific topic of interest or browse through categories, such as computers or sports.

You can access Lycos at the following Web site:

http://www.lycos.com

POINT Lycos offers a connection to **Point**, a search tool that keeps track of the best pages on the Web. You can browse through categories or type in a topic and Point will display the top-ranked pages matching your request.

Yahoo

Yahoo lets you search for a specific topic of interest or browse through categories, such as arts or science.

You can access Yahoo at the following Web site:

http://www.yahoo.com

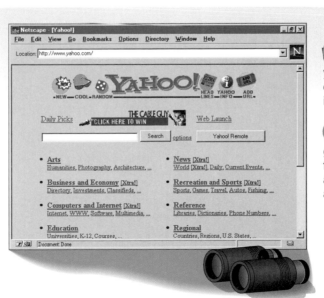

Yahoo has a **Cool** feature that takes you to Web pages Yahoo considers innovative and interesting.

Yahoo also has a **Headlines** feature that gives you up-to-date news for various categories such as entertainment, politics and sports.

CREATE AND PUBLISH WEB PAGES

You can create and publish Web pages to share information with people around the world.

WHY PUBLISH?

Individuals publish on the Web to share their favorite pictures, hobbies and interests.

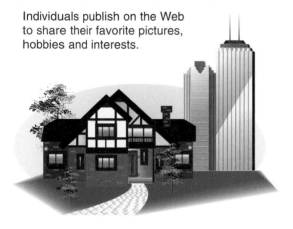

Companies publish on the Web to promote their businesses, advertise products and publicize job openings.

WEB PAGE ORGANIZATION

Home Page

A home page provides a general introduction to your Web pages. A home page often includes a table of contents that describes all of your Web pages.

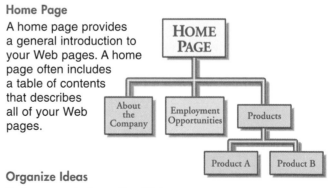

Organize Ideas

Before you start creating Web pages, decide what ideas you will discuss and how the ideas relate to one another. Break up your information so you discuss only one major idea on each page. You may find it helpful to first sketch the design of your pages on paper.

HTML

HyperText Markup Language (HTML)
is a computer language used to
create Web pages.

An HTML document has
the extension .html or .htm
(example: index.html).

Text Editor

You can create HTML documents
using a text editor or word processor.

You enter HTML text commands, called tags,
to define how text and graphics will appear on
a page. Tags usually work in pairs and affect
the text between the tags. For example, the
tags <B>dog</B> will make the text "dog"
appear in **bold**.

HTML Editor

You can also create HTML documents using
HTML editors, such as Microsoft FrontPage
or Netscape Gold.

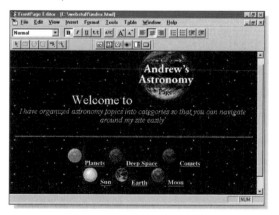

HTML editors make it easier to create Web
pages because they enter tags for you. This
means you do not need to know the HTML
computer language to create Web pages.

CREATE AND PUBLISH WEB PAGES

You can add graphics to your Web pages to make the pages more attractive.

Avoid placing a large number of graphics on your Web pages. Graphics increase the time it takes for pages to appear on the screen.

Create Graphics

You can use a graphics program, such as Adobe Photoshop or Corel PHOTO-PAINT, to create graphics you can add to Web pages.

Copy Graphics

There are places on the Internet that offer graphics you can use on your Web pages. Make sure you have permission to use any graphics you copy from the Internet.

You can also buy a collection of ready-made graphics, called clip art, at most computer stores.

Scan Graphics

You can use a scanner to scan pictures, drawings and logos into a computer. You can then use the scanned images on your Web pages.

LINKS

You can add links
to your Web pages.

Links allow readers to
select highlighted text
or pictures to display
other, related pages
on the Web.

Where to Link

You can place links on your Web
pages that connect to other
pages you have created. This
helps readers flip through your
Web pages.

You can also place links on
your Web pages that connect
to pages maintained by other
organizations. This gives
readers instant access to
related information.

Be Descriptive

Make sure you describe linked
pages accurately so readers will
know whether they want to select
a link. Telling readers to "click
here" is not very informative.

Check Links

Web page addresses
sometimes change. You
should regularly check
all the links on your Web
pages to make sure the
addresses are still correct.

CREATE AND PUBLISH WEB PAGES

PUBLISH WEB PAGES

Once you have created your Web pages, you need to publish the pages so people around the world can view them.

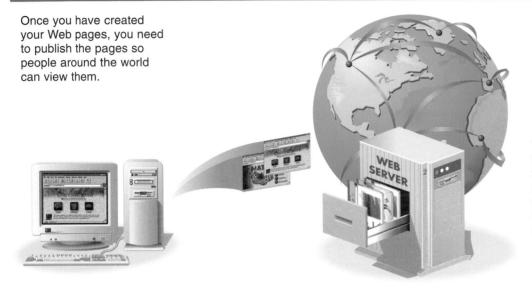

You publish Web pages by transferring the pages to a Web server. A Web server is a computer connected to the Internet that makes your pages available to the world.

Where to Publish Web Pages

The service that connects you to the Internet may offer space on its Web server where you can store your Web pages free of charge. The service may limit the amount of space you can use.

Maintain Web Pages

After you publish Web pages, make sure you keep the information on the pages up-to-date. Incorporate feedback you receive from readers and try to improve the content and design of the pages whenever possible.

PUBLICIZE WEB PAGES

Search Tools

You can use the **Submit It** Web site to announce your Web pages. The **Submit It** site sends information about your Web pages to many different search tools. Search tools help people find pages on the Web. You can access **Submit It** at the following Web site:

http://www.submit-it.com

Exchange Links

If another page on the Web discusses related ideas, ask if they will place a link to your page if you do the same.

Off the Internet

You can publicize your Web page address on business cards and company letterhead. Companies often include Web page addresses in television, radio, newspaper and magazine advertisements.

Web Pages

Many companies set aside areas on their Web pages for advertisements. For a fee, you can use these areas to advertise your Web pages.

Feeling overwhelmed by the amount of information on the Web? This chapter describes 80 interesting sites and provides a good place to start your Web exploration.

CHAPTER 11:

INTERESTING WEB SITES

ARTS AND ENTERTAINMENT

Theater Central

Your one-stop guide to theater on the Internet, complete with job listings, professional contacts and links to other theater-related sites.

 http://www.theatre-central.com

TV Net

Television listings from around the world, links to your favorite shows and more.

URL http://www.tvnet.com

WebMuseum

A huge collection of some of the world's best art.

URL http://www.emf.net/louvre

World Wide Arts Resources

Are you looking for specific art information? Check out this complete guide to art and culture on the Web.

URL http://wwar.com/index.html

CyberDance - Ballet on the Net

A great source of ballet and modern dance information on the Internet.

URL http://www.thepoint.net/~raw/dance.htm

Internet Movie Database

This free source of movie information is the largest of its kind on the Internet.

URL http://us.imdb.com

Internet Underground Music Archive

Considered by many to be the place to go on the Web for all kinds of music information.

URL http://www.iuma.com

Mr. Showbiz

Articles, reviews, the latest news from the entertainment world and much more.

URL http://www.mrshowbiz.com

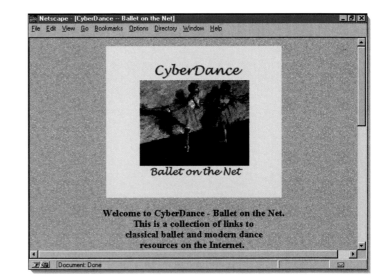

BUSINESS

American Express

Locate American Express offices around the world or book your next trip at this site.

URL http://www.americanexpress.com

American Stock Exchange

Check today's market summary or look back through the past year's archives.

URL http://www.amex.com

CareerMosaic

Many of the world's largest corporations post their open positions at this site.

URL http://www.careermosaic.com/cm

Consumer Information Center

A wealth of online financial and investment information.

URL http://www.pueblo.gsa.gov

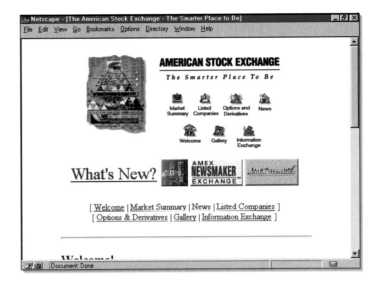

E*TRADE

Trade stocks over the Internet, get stock quotes or play the Stock Market Game.

URL http://www.etrade.com

Online Banking and Financial Services Directory

A list of more than 1000 banks, credit unions, building societies and investment services companies available on the Web.

URL http://www.orcc.com/orcc/banking.htm

VISA Expo

Information and special offers for VISA cardholders around the world.

URL http://www.visa.com

Wall Street Journal Interactive Edition

This continually updated site is the business person's best friend.

URL http://update.wsj.com

FOOD AND DRINK

800 Spirits

Order wines, liqueurs and other goodies online for delivery around the world.

 http://owl.net:80/OWLspace/spirits

Chocolatier Recipe Index

Some of the best and most exotic chocolate recipes in the world are available here, complete with mouth-watering pictures.

 http://www.godiva.com/recipes/chocolatier/index.html

Food Channel

A great starting point for food information, whether you are searching for industry trends, food fun, dining out advice, cooking help or anything else.

 http://www.foodchannel.com/home.html

Ragu

This is a top-notch site with recipes, contests and guides to speaking Italian.

 http://www.eat.com

Republic of Tea

Order a wide variety of teas online and learn how to make the perfect cup of tea.

 http://eMall.Com/Republic/Tea.html

Sugarplums

The culinary magazine offers gourmet recipes and tips as well as a special section on food and romance.

 http://www.sugarplums.com

Star Chefs

Interviews, biographies and recipes from some of the world's top chefs.

 http://starchefs.com

Veggies Unite!

A great collection of vegetarian recipes and cooking tips, a veggie glossary and more.

 http://vegweb.com

HUMOR

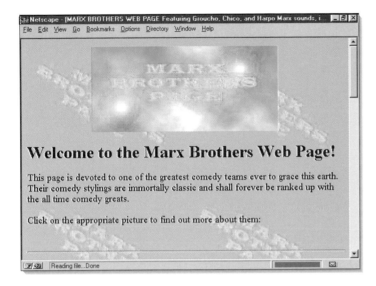

Murphy's Laws

Anything that can go wrong, will go wrong! Check out many more of Murphy's Laws at this site.

URL http://www.pol.pl/humor/murphye.htm

Rec.humor.funny Home Page

Thousands of jokes and humorous stories make this site a popular hangout for cyber-comedians.

URL http://comedy.clari.net/rhf

The Comic Strip

Read comic strips that appear in newspapers nationwide.

URL http://www.unitedmedia.com/comics

Top Ten Lists from the Late Show with David Letterman

You don't have to stay up late to hear the Top Ten! Easily search through all of David's famous nightly lists or take a peek at the favorite lists of the show's writers.

URL http://www.cbs.com/lateshow/ttlist.html

Biggest List of Humor Sites on the Web

This monster list of humorous sites on the Web is a comedy fan's dream come true.

URL http://mars.superlink.net/~zorro/humor.htm

Comedy Central Online

Visit the site of this television comedy channel for a few laughs. Maybe you'd like to try some of Dr. Katz's E-Therapy by filling out the hilarious Auto-Diagnosis Form!

URL http://www.comcentral.com

Courtroom Bloopers

Some of the funniest things ever said or done in front of a judge.

URL http://iquest.com/~fitz/diversions/court.html

Marx Brothers

Lots of pictures, sounds and facts about this very funny comedy team.

URL http://www.internetland.net/~gsumner

NEWS

clnet: The Computer Network

Find out what's coming up next week on this acclaimed cable computer news show or review the transcript from a previous episode.

 http://www.cnet.com/Content/Tv

CNN Interactive

Read the latest headlines, try today's quiz or visit the Video Vault to watch video clips of recent news.

URL http://www.cnn.com

Electronic Newsstand

Browse through many popular magazines and even subscribe to your favorites online.

URL http://www.enews.com

Financial Times

This site makes it easy to follow the world's business, economic and political news.

URL http://www.usa.ft.com

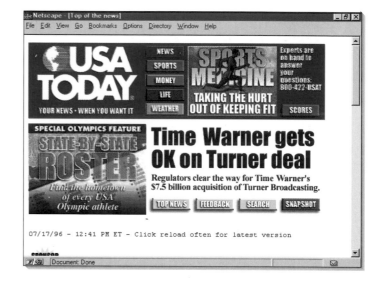

Infoseek Personal

Choose your favorite news topics and have a personalized online newspaper prepared for you daily.

URL http://personal.infoseek.com

NewsPage

Need up-to-date information about a specific industry? Find news on everything from computers to health care at this site.

URL http://www.newspage.com

Online Newspapers

A huge collection of online newspapers from the U.S. and around the world.

URL http://www.ucc.uconn.edu/~jpa94001/papers.html

USA Today

The online version of one of the most popular American national newspapers.

URL http://www.usatoday.com

SCIENCE

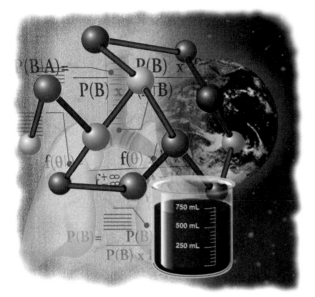

National Space Science Data Center

This site contains a collection of images from space, complete with informative descriptions.

 **URL** http://nssdc.gsfc.nasa.gov

NSF Geosciences Integrated Earth Information Server

This site provides current environmental data from around the world and instructional materials for teachers.

URL http://atm.geo.nsf.gov

Psychology, Behavioral & Brain Sciences

Here you will find journals and other publications in the field of Psychology.

 **URL** http://www.princeton.edu/~harnad

University of Oregon Department of Physics

Don't miss this attractive multimedia site's movies, sounds, animation gallery and more.

URL http://zebu.uoregon.edu

American Chemical Society (ACSWeb)

Information about this society, articles from chemical journals, a software catalog and more.

URL http://www.acs.org

Biologist's Control Panel

This site contains a large collection of biological databases, search tools and other information.

 **URL** http://gc.bcm.tmc.edu:8088/bio

Daily Planet

This site offers information about weather and includes an online guide to meteorology.

URL http://wx3.atmos.uiuc.edu

National Library of Medicine

Access medical and scientific information from this huge library.

  **URL** http://www.nlm.nih.gov

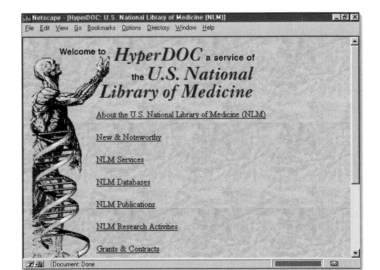

SEARCH TOOLS

AltaVista

Quickly search millions of Web pages and thousands of newsgroups.

 http://altavista.digital.com

Deja News

Calling itself the premier Usenet search utility, Deja News lets you perform simple or detailed searches of all newsgroups.

 http://www.dejanews.com

Four11

Looking for someone on the Internet? Visit Four11 and access over 6.5 million e-mail addresses.

 http://www.four11.com

Infoseek

A diverse search tool that lets you search the Web, newsgroups or e-mail addresses.

 http://www.infoseek.com

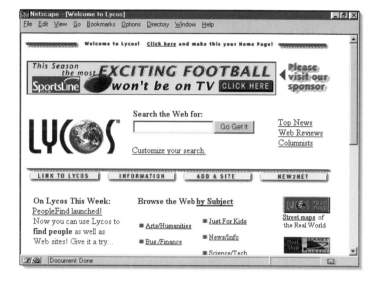

Lycos

Search the Web or check out the directory service from Carnegie Mellon University.

 http://www.lycos.com

Point

Point rates and reviews the best sites on the Web.

 http://www.pointcom.com

Search.com

This site combines hundreds of search tools to help you find anything and everything you need.

 http://www.search.com

Yahoo!

The first popular search tool, Yahoo! provides a colorful guide to the online world.

 http://www.yahoo.com

SHOPPING

Federated Department Stores, Inc.

Find out what's hot in these department stores, which include Macy's, Bloomingdale's and The Bon Marché.

 http://www.federated-fds.com

iMALL

You name it, they've got it—electronics, clothing and even art.

 http://www.imall.com

Internet Shopping Network

With thousands of products available online, this is a great place to find computer and home office equipment, plus a few surprises.

 http://www.internet.net

Shopping Europe

If you appreciate fine English and European products from designers like Christian Dior and Laura Ashley, this online shopping site is for you.

 http://www.virtualeurope.nl

All About Kids

Clothes and accessories for children, from babies to pre-teenagers. Order from the online catalog for shipping in the U.S. and abroad.

 http://allaboutkids.com

Catalog Mart

The easiest and fastest way to get just about any catalog available in the U.S. Choose from over 10,000—and they are all free!

 http://catalog.savvy.com

Consumer Direct Electronics

A busy site with audio, security and entertainment products for the home, along with fax machines, phones, microwaves and more.

 http://www.wholesalece.com

Designers Direct

Fashions from Guess, Calvin Klein and Levi's available online.

 http://www.DesignersDirect.com

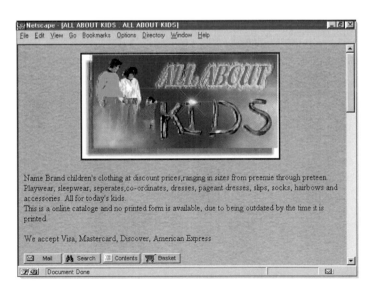

SPORTS

NHL Open Net

Schedules, news, scores, teams, superstars and more from the National Hockey League's official Web site.

URL http://www.nhl.com

Sports Illustrated Online

This site offers sports stories and a sampling of the famous Swimsuit issue.

URL http://www.pathfinder.com/si

Team NFL

The home page of the National Football League.

URL http://www.nflhome.com

The Sports Network

Check out TSN's Web site to find coverage of many sports. Click on "The Playground" to discuss your favorite sport with other fans.

URL http://www.sportsnetwork.com

Baseball Server

Visit this site for detailed information on baseball scores, news and standings, as well as feature articles.

URL http://www2.nando.net/SportsServer/baseball

ESPNET SportsZone

The latest in sports from ESPN, with feature articles, statistics and scores.

URL http://espnet.sportszone.com

golf.com

A top-notch golf site with professional and amateur golf coverage alongside information on golf equipment, schools, resorts and major golf publications.

URL http://www.golf.com

NBA.com

The official site for the National Basketball Association.

URL http://www.nba.com

TRAVEL

Above All Travel

Information and reservations for cruises to Antarctica and Tahiti, hiking and biking expeditions in the Alps and more.

 http://www.aboveall.com

City.Net

This site offers links to information about thousands of destinations around the world.

 http://www.city.net

EarthWise Journeys

From the Amazon to the Yangtse, this is the place to go if you're looking for a vacation that is out of the ordinary.

 http://www.teleport.com/~earthwyz

Internet Cruise Travel Network

A great guide for anyone interested in cruises, with information on everything from day cruises to ocean freighters.

 http://www.cruisetravel.com

Online Vacation Mall™

● Vacation Packages ● Sightseeing Tours ● Vacation Merchandise ● Vacation

Online Vacation Mall

Find a perfect vacation—you can book or cancel your reservations online.

URL http://www.onlinevacationmall.com

Subway Navigator

Find maps for various subway systems around the world. A must-see for fans and users of urban railways.

URL http://metro.jussieu.fr:10001/bin/cities/english

Travel Channel Online Network

Get away from it all! This site offers travel tips and expert advice as well as program information.

URL http://www.travelchannel.com

TravelWeb

Choose from thousands of hotels around the world and make a reservation online.

URL http://www.travelweb.com/index.html

What is electronic mail? This chapter introduces you to electronic mail and teaches you how to create and send messages.

ELECTRONIC MAIL

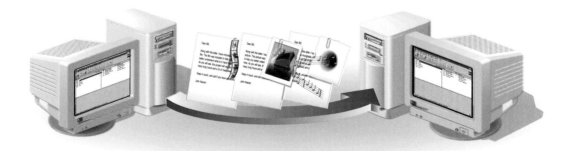

INTRODUCTION TO E-MAIL

You can exchange electronic mail (e-mail) with people around the world.

E-mail provides a fast, economical and convenient way to send messages to family, friends and colleagues.

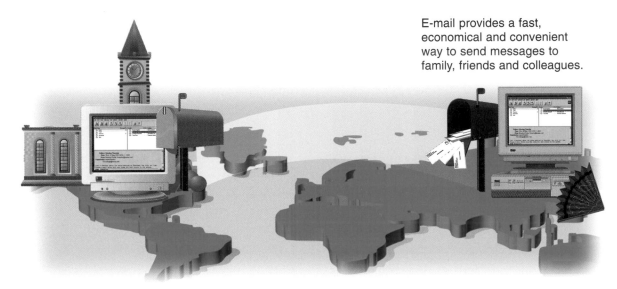

E-mail is much faster than old-fashioned mail, called "snail mail." An e-mail message can travel around the world in minutes.

Once you pay a service provider for a connection to the Internet, there is no charge for sending and receiving e-mail. You do not have to pay extra even if you send a long message or the message travels around the world.

Exchanging e-mail can save you money on long distance calls. The next time you are about to pick up the telephone, consider sending an e-mail message instead.

E-MAIL PROGRAMS

An e-mail program lets
you send, receive and
manage your e-mail
messages.

POPULAR E-MAIL PROGRAMS

Popular e-mail programs include
Eudora Light and Netscape Mail.

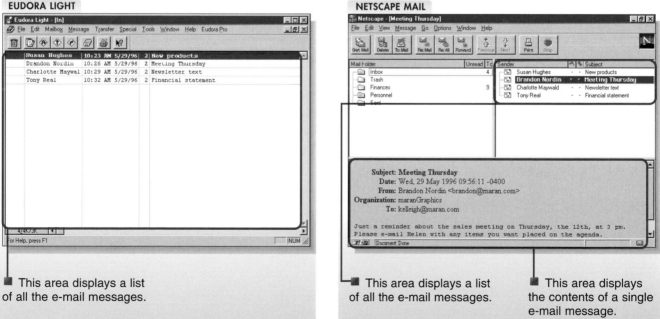

EUDORA LIGHT

■ This area displays a list
of all the e-mail messages.

NETSCAPE MAIL

■ This area displays a list
of all the e-mail messages.

■ This area displays
the contents of a single
e-mail message.

E-MAIL ADDRESSES

You can send a message to anyone around the world if you know the person's e-mail address.

An e-mail address defines the location of an individual's mailbox on the Internet.

PARTS OF AN E-MAIL ADDRESS

An e-mail address consists of two parts separated by the @ ("at") symbol. An e-mail address cannot contain spaces.

■ The **user name** is the name of the person's account. This can be a real name or a nickname.

■ The **domain name** is the location of the person's account on the Internet. Periods (.) separate the various parts of the domain name.

FAMOUS E-MAIL ADDRESSES

NAME	ADDRESS
Bill Gates	billg@microsoft.com
Brad Pitt	ciaobox@msn.com
Madonna	Madonna@wbr.com
President	president@whitehouse.gov
Tom Brokaw	nightly@nbc.com
Tom Clancy	tomclancy@aol.com

ORGANIZATION OR COUNTRY

The last few characters in an e-mail address usually indicate the type of organization or country to which the person belongs.

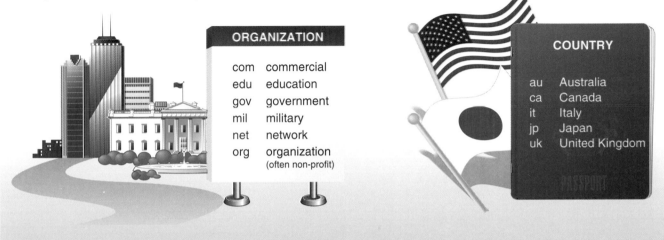

ORGANIZATION

com	commercial
edu	education
gov	government
mil	military
net	network
org	organization (often non-profit)

COUNTRY

au	Australia
ca	Canada
it	Italy
jp	Japan
uk	United Kingdom

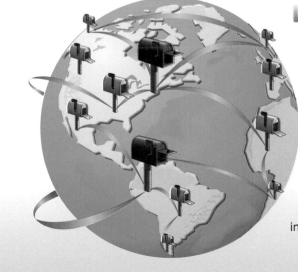

FIND E-MAIL ADDRESSES

There is no central listing of e-mail addresses. The best way to find the e-mail addresses of friends or colleagues is to phone them and ask.

There are many places on the Web that help you search for e-mail addresses free of charge. The following Web site lists various places that allow you to search for e-mail addresses:

http://home.netscape.com/home/internet-white-pages.html

CREATE A MESSAGE

Make sure every message you send is clear, concise and contains no spelling or grammar errors. Also make sure the message will not be misinterpreted. For example, the reader may not realize a statement is meant to be sarcastic.

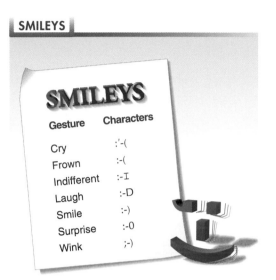

You can use special characters, called smileys or emoticons, to express emotions in messages. These characters resemble human faces if you turn them sideways.

ABBREVIATIONS

Abbreviations are commonly used in messages to save time typing.

Abbreviation	Meaning	Abbreviation	Meaning
BTW	by the way	LOL	laughing out loud
FAQ	frequently asked questions	MOTAS	member of the appropriate sex
FOAF	friend of a friend	MOTOS	member of the opposite sex
FWIW	for what it's worth		
FYI	for your information	MOTSS	member of the same sex
IMHO	in my humble opinion		
		ROTFL	rolling on the floor laughing
IMO	in my opinion		
IOW	in other words	SO	significant other
L8R	later	WRT	with respect to

SHOUTING

A MESSAGE WRITTEN IN CAPITAL LETTERS IS ANNOYING AND HARD TO READ. THIS IS CALLED SHOUTING.

Always use upper and lower case letters when typing messages.

FLAME

A flame is an angry or insulting message directed at one person. A flame war is an argument that continues for a while. Avoid starting or participating in flame wars.

SIGNATURE

You can have an e-mail program add information about yourself to the end of every message you send. This prevents you from having to type the same information over and over again.

A signature can include your name, e-mail address, occupation or favorite quotation. You can also use plain characters to display simple pictures. Do not create a signature that is more than four lines long.

PARTS OF A MESSAGE

From:

Address of the person sending the message.

To:

Address of the person receiving the message.

Subject:

Identifies the contents of the message. Make sure your subject is informative. Do not use subjects such as "For your information" or "Read this now."

From:	mary@sales.abc.com
To:	john@maran.com
Subject:	Sales Awards
Cc:	sarah@sales.abc.com
Bcc:	karen@abc.com

Congratulations on your achievement! I'm looking forward to seeing you at the awards ceremony!

Cc:

Stands for carbon copy. A carbon copy is an exact copy of a message. You can send a carbon copy of a message to a person who is not directly involved, but would be interested in the message.

Bcc:

Stands for blind carbon copy. This lets you send the same message to several people without them knowing that others have also received the same message.

ATTACH FILES TO MESSAGES

You can attach a document, picture, sound, video or program to a message you are sending.

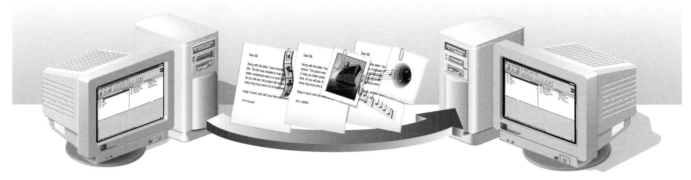

Many e-mail programs use Multipurpose Internet Mail Extensions (MIME) to attach files to messages.

To view an attached file, the computer receiving the message must be able to understand MIME. The computer must also have a program that can view or play the file.

COMPRESS ATTACHED FILES

When you want to attach a large file to an e-mail message, you can save time and money by compressing the file. Compressing a file shrinks the file to a smaller size. This allows the file to transfer more quickly over the Internet.

You can also use a compression program to combine numerous files into a single file. This means you do not need to attach each file individually to an e-mail message.

The person receiving a compressed file must use a decompression program to expand the file to its original form.

SEND A MESSAGE

**You can send a message
to exchange ideas or
request information.**

If you want to
practice sending
a message, send
a message to
yourself.

When you send a message,
do not assume the person will
read the message right
away. Some people may
not regularly check their
messages.

COMPOSE OFFLINE

You can write e-mail messages when you
are not connected to the Internet (offline).
When you finish writing all your messages,
you can connect and send the messages
all at once. This saves you money since
you do not have to pay for the time
you spend composing
messages.

USE THE ADDRESS BOOK

An e-mail program provides an address
book where you can store the addresses
of people you frequently send messages
to. An address book saves you from
having to type the same addresses
over and over again.

SEND PRIVATE MESSAGES

There are ways to send messages privately over the Internet. This protects messages from crackers who illegally break into computer systems for fun or to steal information.

Pretty Good Privacy

Pretty Good Privacy (PGP) is a program widely used to send e-mail messages privately over the Internet. PGP is very controversial since no one, not even the government, can crack the code. The PGP program is available for free on the Internet.

Privacy Enhanced Mail

Privacy Enhanced Mail (PEM) is another program designed to keep e-mail messages private.

BOUNCED MESSAGES

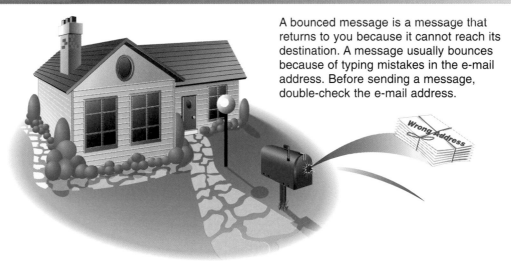

A bounced message is a message that returns to you because it cannot reach its destination. A message usually bounces because of typing mistakes in the e-mail address. Before sending a message, double-check the e-mail address.

E-MAIL FEATURES

RECEIVE MESSAGES

You do not have to be at your computer to receive a message. Your service provider keeps all your messages until you retrieve them. Make sure you regularly check for messages.

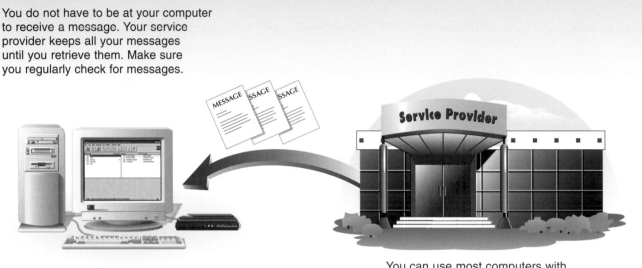

You can use most computers with a modem to connect to your service provider and retrieve messages. This means you can retrieve your messages when traveling.

REPLY TO A MESSAGE

You can reply to a message to answer a question, express an opinion or supply additional information.

When you reply to a message, make sure you include part of the original message. This is called quoting. Quoting helps the reader identify which message you are replying to. To save the reader time, make sure you delete all parts of the original message that do not directly relate to your reply.

FORWARD A MESSAGE

After reading a message, you can add comments and then send the message to a friend or colleague.

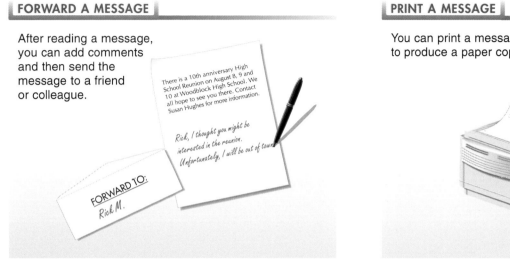

PRINT A MESSAGE

You can print a message to produce a paper copy.

ORGANIZE MESSAGES

E-mail programs usually store messages you have sent, received and deleted in separate folders. This helps you keep messages organized so you can review them later.

You can also create personalized folders to better organize your messages.

Make sure you clean out your folders on a regular basis by deleting messages you no longer need.

What are mailing lists and why would you want to join them? This chapter introduces you to the different types of mailing lists and provides helpful tips on what to do once you have joined.

MAILING LISTS

INTRODUCTION TO MAILING LISTS

A mailing list is a discussion group that uses e-mail to communicate.

There are thousands of mailing lists that cover a wide variety of topics, from aromatherapy to Led Zeppelin. New mailing lists are created every week.

HOW MAILING LISTS WORK

When a mailing list receives a message, a copy of the message goes to everyone on the mailing list.

Most mailing lists let you send and receive messages. Some mailing lists only let you receive messages, not send them.

FIND MAILING LISTS

You can find a list of mailing lists at the following Web site:

http://www.neosoft.com/internet/paml

You can search for mailing lists that discuss a specific topic at the following Web site:

http://www.liszt.com

INTERESTING MAILING LISTS

A Word A Day
Sends you a word and its definition every day.

Contact: wsmith@wordsmith.org
Type in subject line: subscribe Your Name

Homebrew
Discussion of beer and other fermented beverages.

Contact: homebrew-request@hpfcmi.fc.hp.com
Type in message: subscribe

Choco
Sends you a collection of chocolate recipes once a month.

Contact: majordomo@apk.net
Type in message: subscribe choco

Joke of the Day!
Sends you a joke at least once a week.

Contact: majordomo@gnt.net
Type in message: info joke

Dinosaur
Discussion of dinosaurs and other prehistoric animals.
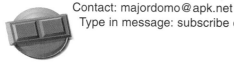
Contact: listproc@usc.edu
Type in message: subscribe dinosaur Your Name

Kids Books
Reviews of children's books.

Contact: kidsbooks-request@armory.com
Type in message: subscribe

Golf Discussion List
Discussion of the game of golf.

Contact: listserv@ubvm.cc.buffalo.edu
Type in message: subscribe GOLF-L

Melrose Place
Discussion of the popular television series.
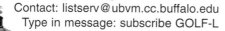
Contact:
melrose-place-request@ferkel.ucsb.edu
Type in message: subscribe

SUBSCRIBE TO A MAILING LIST

Just as you would subscribe to a newspaper or magazine, you can subscribe to a mailing list that interests you.

Subscribing adds your e-mail address to the mailing list.

Mailing List
Subscribe Here!

chris@xyz.com
ben@bookstore.com
carl@sales.abc.com
david@maran.com
jack@123.com

e-mail addresses

andrew@iog.com
christie@mss.com
julie@bcb.com
noel@ber.com
tamara@vox.com
russ@wav.com
susan@123.com

Unsubscribe

If you no longer want to receive messages from a mailing list, you can unsubscribe from the mailing list at any time. Unsubscribing removes your e-mail address from the mailing list.

MAILING LIST ADDRESSES

Each mailing list has two addresses. Make sure you send your messages to the appropriate address.

Mailing List Address

The mailing list address receives messages intended for the entire mailing list. This is the address you use to send messages you want all the people on the list to receive. Do not send subscription or unsubscription requests to the mailing list address.

Mailing List

Administrative

Administrative Address

The administrative address receives messages dealing with administrative issues. This is the address you use to subscribe to or unsubscribe from a mailing list.

Welcome Message

When you subscribe to a mailing list, you usually receive a welcome message to confirm that your e-mail address has been added to the list. This message may explain any rules the mailing list has about sending messages to the list.

Check for Messages

After you subscribe to a mailing list, make sure you check your mailbox frequently. You can receive dozens of messages in a short period of time.

Digests

If you receive a lot of messages from a mailing list, find out if the list is available as a digest. A digest groups individual messages together and sends them to you as one message.

Vacations

When you go on vacation, make sure you temporarily unsubscribe from all your mailing lists. This will prevent your mailbox from overflowing with messages.

TYPES OF MAILING LISTS

MANUALLY MAINTAINED LISTS

A person manages a manually maintained mailing list.

A manually maintained list usually contains the word "request" in its e-mail address (example: hang-gliding-request@lists.utah.edu).

Join a List

When you want to join a manually maintained list, make sure you find out what information the administrator needs and include the information in your message.

AUTOMATED LISTS

A computer program manages an automated mailing list. There are three popular programs that manage automated lists—listproc, listserv and majordomo.

An automated list typically contains the name of the program that manages the list in its e-mail address (example: majordomo@teleport.com).

Anna Brown	annab@sales.maran.com
David Jones	davidj@mustang.net
Debbie LeRoy	dleroy@med.nyu.edu
Chris McKenzie	chrism@magic.org
John Smith	jsmith@stay.com
Mary Vickers	mvickers@company.com
Pete Lilly	plilly@maran.com
June Burke	jburke@abc.com
Andrea Bartell	abartell@sales.abc.com

Join a List

When you want to join an automated list, make sure you find out what information the program needs and include the information in your message. If a program does not understand your message, it may not respond to your request.

MAILING LIST RESTRICTIONS

RESTRICTED MAILING LISTS

Some mailing lists restrict the number of people allowed to join the list. If you want to join one of these lists, you may have to wait for someone else to leave the list.

Other mailing lists require that you meet certain qualifications to join the list. For example, a mailing list about surgery may be restricted to medical doctors.

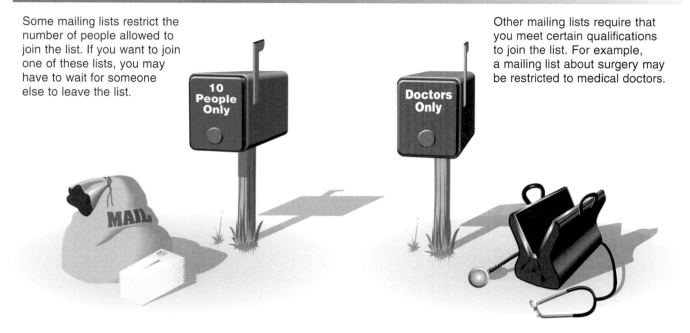

MODERATED MAILING LISTS

Some mailing lists are moderated. A volunteer reads each message sent to a moderated list and decides if the message is appropriate for the list. If the message is appropriate, the volunteer sends the message to every person on the mailing list.

A moderated mailing list keeps discussions on topic and removes messages containing ideas already discussed.

In an unmoderated mailing list, all messages are automatically sent to everyone on the list.

MAILING LIST ETIQUETTE

Mailing list etiquette refers to the proper way to behave when sending messages to a mailing list.

READ MESSAGES

Read the messages in a mailing list for a week before sending a message. This is a good way to learn how people in a mailing list communicate and prevents you from submitting inappropriate information or information already discussed.

WRITING STYLE

Hundreds of people may read a message you send to a mailing list. Before sending a message, make sure you carefully reread the message.

Make sure your message is clear, concise and contains no spelling or grammar errors.

Also make sure your message will not be misinterpreted. For example, not all readers will realize a statement is meant to be sarcastic.

> ## MESSAGE
>
> I found a flower in my bakyard and I want to identify it. It's sort of tall, colored blue and purple, maybe with red dots on it's leaves. If anyone can help me, I'd appreciate it.
>
> ⟲ -Spelling mistakes
> ? -Unclear

SUBJECT

The subject of a message is the first item people read. Make sure the subject clearly identifies the contents of the message. For example, the subject "Read this now" or "For your information" is not very informative.

Dinosaur Fossil Found

I just returned from a dig open to the public in Arizona. I unearthed what was confi... as a T-Rex tooth fragmen... suggestions as to the val... the item or where I cou... it examined here in A...

Chocolate Mousse Recipe

My recipe for chocolate mouss... says that I should fold the cho... mixture into the whipped cre... How does one fold chocola... Please help me.

Records For Sale

Anyone still into disco? I have original vinyl recordings of Blondie, KC and the Sunshine Band and ABBA for sale!

REPLY TO MESSAGES

You can reply to a message to answer a question, express an opinion or supply additional information. Reply to a message only when you have something important to say. A reply such as "Me too" or "I agree" is not very informative.

Original Message

I'm planning a trip to Rome this year. Any suggestions for sights I should see?

Reply

I'm planning a trip to Rome this year. Any suggestions for sights I should see?

I really liked the ancient Forum and the Colosseum.

Quoting

When you reply to a message, make sure you include some of the original message. This is called quoting. Quoting helps readers identify which message you are replying to. To save readers time, make sure you delete all parts of the original message that do not directly relate to your reply.

Private Replies

If your reply would not be of interest to others in a mailing list or if you want to send a private response, send a message to the author instead of sending your reply to the entire mailing list.

John Smith

What is a newsgroup? How do I chat on the Internet? This chapter shows you how to chat and use newsgroups to discuss issues of interest, meet new people and talk to friends and colleagues around the world.

rec.sport.basketball.pro

CHAPTER 14:

NEWSGROUPS AND CHAT

INTRODUCTION TO NEWSGROUPS

A newsgroup is a discussion group that allows people with common interests to communicate with each other.

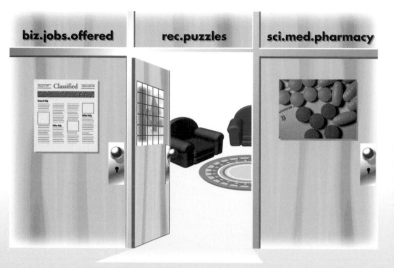

There are thousands of newsgroups on every subject imaginable. Each newsgroup discusses a particular topic such as jobs offered, puzzles or medicine.

Usenet, short for Users' Network, refers to all the computers that distribute newsgroup information.

NEWSGROUP NAMES

The name of a newsgroup describes the type of information discussed in the newsgroup. A newsgroup name consists of two or more words, separated by dots(.).

The first word describes the main topic (example: rec for recreation). Each of the following words narrows the topic.

ARTICLES

A newsgroup can contain hundreds
or thousands of articles.

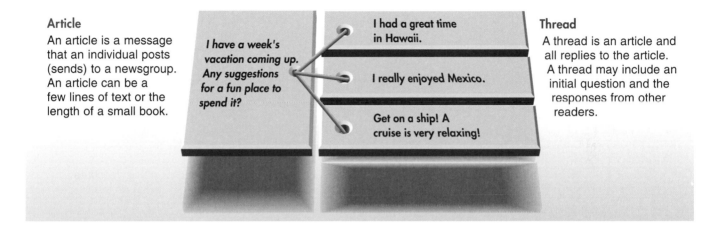

Article

An article is a message
that an individual posts
(sends) to a newsgroup.
An article can be a
few lines of text or the
length of a small book.

I have a week's vacation coming up. Any suggestions for a fun place to spend it?

I had a great time in Hawaii.

I really enjoyed Mexico.

Get on a ship! A cruise is very relaxing!

Thread

A thread is an article and
all replies to the article.
A thread may include an
initial question and the
responses from other
readers.

NEWSREADER

A newsreader is a program
that lets you read and post
articles to newsgroups.

Netscape Navigator comes
with a built-in newsreader,
called Netscape News. Other
popular newsreaders include
News Xpress and Free Agent.

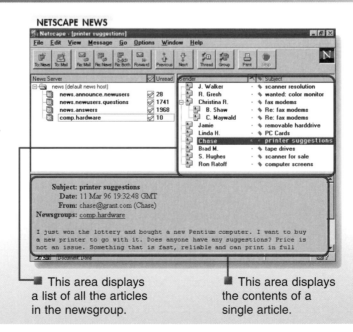

NETSCAPE NEWS

■ This area displays
a list of all the articles
in the newsgroup.

■ This area displays
the contents of a
single article.

SUBSCRIBE TO NEWSGROUPS

You subscribe to a newsgroup you want to read on a regular basis.

If you no longer want to read the articles in a newsgroup, you can unsubscribe from the newsgroup at any time.

MODERATED NEWSGROUPS

Some newsgroups are moderated. In these newsgroups, a volunteer reads each article and decides if the article is appropriate for the newsgroup. If the article is appropriate, the volunteer posts the article for everyone to read.

Moderated newsgroups may have the word "moderated" at the end of the newsgroup name (example: sci.military.moderated).

In an unmoderated newsgroup, all articles are automatically posted for everyone to read.

MAIN NEWSGROUP CATEGORIES

alt (alternative)
General interest discussions that can include unusual or bizarre topics.

Examples
alt.fan.actors
alt.music.alternative
alt.ufo.reports

biz (business)
Business discussions that are usually more commercial in nature than those in other newsgroups. Advertising is allowed and lists of job openings are available.

Examples
biz.books.technical
biz.jobs.offered
biz.marketplace.computers.discussion

comp (computers)
Discussions of computer hardware, software and computer science.

Examples
comp.lang.pascal.borland
comp.security.misc
comp.sys.laptops

K12 (kindergarten to grade 12)
Discussions of topics concerning kindergarten to grade 12 students.

Examples
k12.chat.elementary
k12.ed.life-skills
k12.ed.math

MAIN NEWSGROUP CATEGORIES

misc (miscellaneous)
Discussions of various topics that may overlap topics discussed in other categories.

Examples
misc.consumers.house
misc.entrepreneurs
misc.taxes

news
Discussions about newsgroups in general. Topics range from information about the newsgroup network to advice on how to use it.

Examples
news.admin.misc
news.announce.newgroups
news.newsites

rec (recreation)
Discussions of recreational activities and hobbies.

Examples
rec.arts.movies.reviews
rec.food.recipes
rec.sport.football.pro

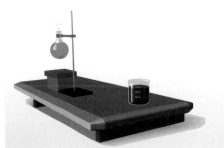

sci (science)
Discussions about science, including research, applied science and the social sciences.

Examples
sci.agriculture
sci.energy
sci.virtual-worlds

soc (social)

Discussions of social issues, including world cultures and political topics.

Examples

soc.college
soc.culture.caribbean
soc.politics

talk

Debates and long discussions, often about controversial subjects.

Examples

talk.environment
talk.philosophy.misc
talk.rumors

REGIONAL NEWSGROUPS

There are newsgroup categories that focus on topics of interest to people living in specific geographical regions.

Examples

aus	Australia
bc	British Columbia
ca	California

NEWSGROUPS FOR BEGINNERS

There are three newsgroups that are helpful for beginners.

Examples

news.announce.newusers
news.answers
news.newusers.questions

WORK WITH ARTICLES

READ AN ARTICLE

You can read articles to learn the opinions and ideas of thousands of people around the world.

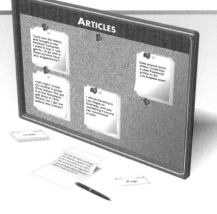

New articles are sent to newsgroups every day. You can browse through articles of interest just as you would browse through the morning paper.

PRINT AN ARTICLE

You can produce a paper copy of an article you find interesting.

POST AN ARTICLE

You can post (send) a new article to a newsgroup to ask a question or express an opinion. Thousands of people around the world may read an article you post.

If you want to practice posting an article, send an article to the **alt.test** newsgroup. You will receive automated replies to let you know you posted correctly. Do not send practice articles to other newsgroups.

REPLY TO AN ARTICLE

You can reply to an article to answer a question, express an opinion or supply additional information.

Reply to an article only when you have something important to say. A reply such as "Me too" or "I agree" is not very informative.

Original Article

The baked potatoes that I serve to my guests are not very appetizing. How can I make them more appealing?

Reply

The baked potatoes that I serve to my guests are not very appetizing. How can I make them more appealing?

Try adding sour cream and paprika, and then sprinkle chili powder on top. Bon appetit!

Quoting

When you reply to an article, make sure you include part of the original article. This is called quoting. Quoting helps readers identify which article you are replying to. To save readers time, make sure you delete all parts of the original article that do not directly relate to your reply.

Private Replies

You can send a reply to the author of an article, the entire newsgroup, or both.

If your reply would not be of interest to others in a newsgroup or if you want to send a private response, send a message to the author instead of posting your reply to the entire newsgroup.

ENCODE ARTICLES

UUENCODE

An article can contain information other than text, such as a graphic or sound recording. To send this type of information to a newsgroup, you need to use uuencode software. Uuencode software lets you convert a graphic or sound recording so it can travel across the Internet.

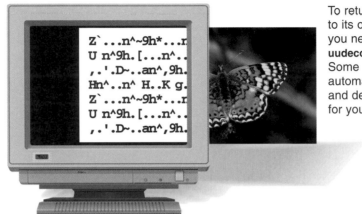

To return information to its original format, you need to use **uudecode** software. Some newsreaders automatically encode and decode information for you.

ROT13

ROT13 lets you turn a newsgroup article you post into a string of meaningless characters. This prevents others from reading information that may be offensive or a spoiler, such as the ending of a movie.

ROT13 works by transposing each letter in an article by 13 characters. For example, the letter "a" becomes the letter "n."

Gur raqvat bs gur zbivr vf vaperqvoyr! Wnpbo naq Anapl svanyyl ernpu gur gbc bs Zbhag Rirerfg, naq ur cebcbfrf gb ure. Anapl npprcgf!

The ending of the movie is incredible! Jacob and Nancy finally reach the top of Mount Everest, and he proposes to her. Nancy accepts!

If you want to read an article encoded using ROT13, you must first decode the text. Some news readers can decode articles for you.

NEWS SERVER

A news server is a computer that stores newsgroup articles.

News servers are maintained by service providers, which are companies that give you access to the Internet.

When you send an article to a newsgroup, the news server you are connected to keeps a copy of the article and then distributes the article to other news servers around the world.

Each news server has an administrator who may select newsgroups based on what the administrator believes to be appropriate for the readers. Limiting the available newsgroups saves valuable storage space on the news server.

After a few days or weeks, articles are removed from a news server to make room for new articles. When you see an article you want to keep, make sure you print or save the article.

261

NEWSGROUP ETIQUETTE

Newsgroup etiquette refers to the proper way to behave when sending messages to a newsgroup.

WRITING STYLE

Thousands of people around the world may read an article you post to a newsgroup. Before posting an article, make sure you carefully reread the article.

ARTICLE

I just won the lottery. I bought a new Pentium computer. I want to buy a new printer to go with it. Does anyone has any suggestions? Price is probably not an issue but it might be. I would prefer something that are fast, reliable and can print in full color. Thanks in advance.

⟨ -Grammar errors

? -Misleading

Make sure your article is clear, concise and contains no spelling or grammar errors.

Also make sure your article will not be misinterpreted. For example, not all readers will realize a statement is meant to be sarcastic.

SUBJECT

The subject of an article is the first item people read. Make sure your subject clearly identifies the contents of your article. For example, the subject "Read this now" or "For your information" is not very informative.

Expensive Fishing Equipment

I really enjoy fishing, but all of my equipment is relatively inexpensive. My fishing buddies keep telling me to upgrade. Will costly reels and lures actually make a difference? Is good technique more important than spending lots of money?

B.J. Wilson

Hot Springs in Arkansas

My wife and I are planning to take a trip through Arkansas next year. We've heard there are some lovely hot springs in the state, but we don't know where. Could someone please give us some advice?

Thanks, Mark C.

Mountain Bike Tune-ups

This is my first year of mountain biking, and so far I've been doing my own tune-ups. But lately my bike hasn't performed well. For example, the chain slips when I switch gears. I'm wondering if I should pay a mechanic to do my tune-ups. Is it worth it?

Thanks, Ronald Hill

READ ARTICLES

Read the articles in a newsgroup for a week before posting an article. This is called lurking. Lurking is a good way to learn how people in a newsgroup communicate and prevents you from posting information others have already read.

READ THE FAQ

The FAQ (Frequently Asked Questions) is a document that contains a list of questions and answers that often appear in a newsgroup.

The FAQ prevents new readers from asking questions that have already been asked. Make sure you read the FAQ before posting any articles to a newsgroup.

POST TO THE APPROPRIATE NEWSGROUP

Make sure you post an article to the appropriate newsgroup. This ensures that people interested in your questions and comments will see your article.

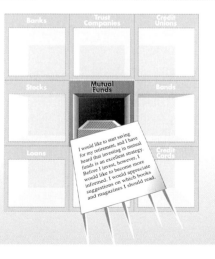

Do not post an article to several inappropriate newsgroups. This is called spamming. Spamming is particularly annoying when the article serves a commercial purpose, such as selling a product or service.

CHAT

You can instantly communicate with people around the world by typing back and forth. This is called chatting.

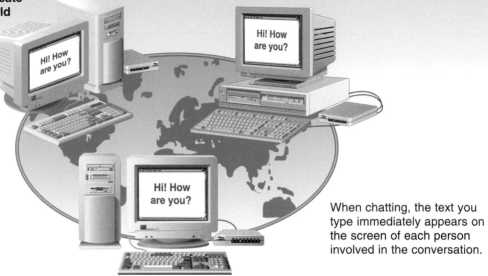

Chatting is a great way to meet people and exchange ideas.

When chatting, the text you type immediately appears on the screen of each person involved in the conversation.

SAVE MONEY

You can use the chat feature to communicate with family, friends and colleagues in other cities, states or countries without paying long distance telephone charges.

NICKNAMES

People participating in a conversation often choose nicknames. Do not assume people are really who they say they are.

CHANNELS

There are different chat rooms, or channels, that you can join. Each channel usually focuses on a specific topic. The name of a channel often tells you the theme of the discussion.

Celebrities sometimes make publicized appearances on specific chat channels.

CHATTING ON THE INTERNET

Internet Relay Chat (IRC) is a popular chatting system on the Internet. IRC lets you chat privately or in groups. Popular IRC channels include 30+, Friendly and Hot Tub.

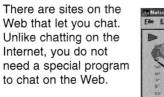

You need an IRC program to participate in IRC chats. You can get an IRC program at the following Web sites:

Global Chat
http://www.qdeck.com/chat/download.html

mIRC
http://www.emapnet.com/service/mirc/download.html

CHATTING ON THE WEB

There are sites on the Web that let you chat. Unlike chatting on the Internet, you do not need a special program to chat on the Web.

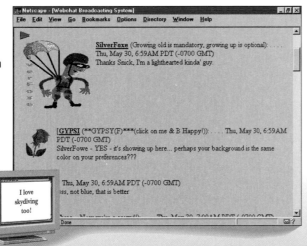

WebChat was the first chatting application on the Web and is still the most heavily trafficked Web site. There are hundreds of WebChat channels you can join. Popular channels include those designed for specific age groups, such as Pre-Teen Chat, Thirtysomething and Fifty Plus Chat.

You can chat on the Web at the following site:

WebChat
http://wbs.net

CHAT

3-D CHAT

You can meet people on the Internet by walking through three-dimensional rooms and chatting with people you encounter.

You need a special program to experience 3-D chat. You can get 3-D chat programs at the following Web sites:

Virtual Places
http://www.vplaces.com/index.htm

Worlds Chat
http://www.worlds.net/wc

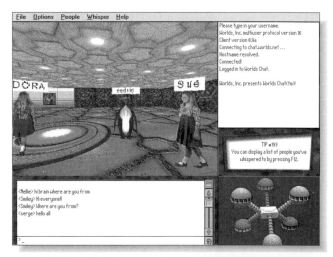

Choose an Avatar

An avatar is an object that represents you in a 3-D chat room.

You can choose from many types of avatars, including a person, fish or butterfly.

Move Through Rooms

You can use your mouse or arrow keys to move through rooms. You can walk through hallways and move closer to people who interest you.

You need a sound card and speakers to listen to music and sound effects while moving through three-dimensional rooms.

TALKING OVER THE INTERNET

Like talking on the telephone, you can talk to people over the Internet. Talking over the Internet lets you hear the voices of family, friends and colleagues around the world without paying any long distance telephone charges.

Hi! How are you? The weather here is hot & sunny. We have had this great weather for about two weeks now! How is It over there?

Equipment

You need a sound card, microphone, speakers and at least a 14,400 bps modem to talk to another person over the Internet.

A half-duplex sound card only lets one person talk at a time. A full-duplex sound card lets two people talk at once, just as you would talk on the telephone.

Programs

Netscape version 3.0 includes a feature called CoolTalk, which lets you talk to people over the Internet. You can get other popular programs that allow you to talk over the Internet at the following Web sites:

Internet Phone
http://www.vocaltec.com/products.htm

WebTalk
http://www.quarterdeck.com/qdeck/products/webtalk

What is FTP? This chapter introduces you to FTP and describes the different types of files you can copy to your computer.

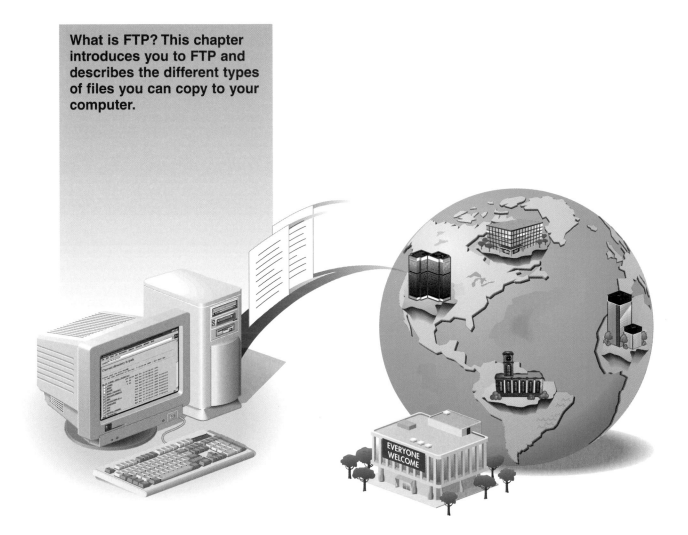

FTP

INTRODUCTION TO FTP

File Transfer Protocol (FTP) lets you look through files stored on computers around the world and copy files that interest you.

FTP SITE

An FTP site is a place on the Internet that stores files. FTP sites are maintained by colleges, universities, government agencies, companies and individuals. There are thousands of FTP sites scattered across the Internet.

Private FTP Site

Some FTP sites are private and require you to enter a password before you can access any files. Many corporations maintain private FTP sites to make files available to their employees and clients around the world.

Anonymous FTP Site

Many FTP sites are anonymous. Anonymous FTP sites let you access files without entering a password. These sites store huge collections of files that anyone can copy (download) free of charge.

HOW FILES ARE STORED

Files at FTP sites are stored in different directories.

Just as folders organize documents in a filing cabinet, directories organize information at an FTP site.

■ **File Names**

Every file stored at an FTP site has a name and an extension, separated by a period. The name describes the contents of a file. The extension usually identifies the type of file.

manual.txt

Development in the Western sense is to economy. Third World production especially order to c on the W kind of de however, costly ma expensiv operation

porsche.gif

THE FTP SCREEN

```
Netscape - [Directory of /pub]
File  Edit  View  Go  Bookmarks  Options  Directory  Window  Help
Location: ftp://ftp.loc.gov/pub/

Current directory is /pub

Please read the file README
it was last modified on Wed Dec  7 10:43:49 1994 - 527 days ago

Up to higher level directory
  .names                144 bytes Wed Oct 19 00:00:00 1994
  INDEX                  83 Kb    Wed Dec 07 00:00:00 1994
  README                  5 Kb    Wed Dec 07 00:00:00 1994
  about.internet/                 Thu May 09 11:47:00 1996 Directory
  american.memory/                Tue Apr 23 09:15:00 1996 Directory
  cds/                            Wed Jan 17 09:33:00 1996 Directory
  collections.s...                Fri Jan 19 09:34:00 1996 Directory
  copyright/                      Thu Apr 18 17:42:00 1996 Directory
  crs/                            Mon Nov 20 08:12:00 1995 Directory
  ead/                            Mon Feb 26 16:52:00 1996 Directory
  exhibit.images/                 Wed Oct 12 00:00:00 1994 Directory
Document: Done
```

■ The files you want to copy to your computer are usually in the pub (public) directory.

■ Most well-established FTP sites include files that describe the rest of the files offered at the site. Look for files named "readme" or "index."

POPULAR FTP SITES

Some popular FTP sites include:	
Library of Congress	ftp://ftp.loc.gov
Microsoft Corporation	ftp://ftp.microsoft.com
SunSITE	ftp://sunsite.unc.edu
Washington University	ftp://wuarchive.wustl.edu
Wiretap Library	ftp://wiretap.spies.com

The following Web site displays a list of most FTP sites:

http://hoohoo.ncsa.uiuc.edu/ftp-interface.html

TYPES OF FILES

TEXT

You can get interesting documents for research and for enjoyment. You can obtain books, journals, electronic magazines, computer manuals, government documents, news summaries and academic papers. Look for these extensions:

.asc .doc .htm .html
.msg .txt .wpd

GRAPHICS

You can get graphics, such as computer-generated art, museum paintings and pictures of famous people. Look for these extensions:

.bmp .eps .gif .jpg
.pict .png

SOUND

You can get theme songs, sound effects, clips of famous speeches and lines from television shows and movies. Look for these extensions:

.au .ra .ram .snd .wav

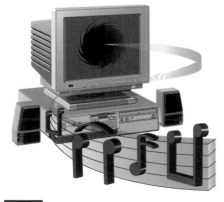

VIDEO

You can get movie clips, cartoons, educational videos and computer-generated animation. Look for these extensions:

.avi .mov .mpg

PROGRAMS

You can get programs to use on your computer, such as word processors, spreadsheets, databases, games and much more. Look for these extensions:

.bat   .com   .exe

Public Domain

Public domain programs are free and have no copyright restrictions. You can change and distribute public domain programs as you wish.

Freeware

Freeware programs are free, but have copyright restrictions. The author may require you to follow certain rules if you want to change or distribute freeware programs.

**Free!
(with restrictions)**

◆ You must include the author's name (and this file) wherever the program is distributed.

◆ You must not sell this program.

◆ You must n̶o̶t̶ ̶b̶a̶n̶d̶ ̶t̶h̶i̶s̶ program in

◆ You must registrati

Shareware

You can try a shareware program free of charge for a limited time. If you like the program and want to continue using it, you must pay the author of the program.

FTP TIPS

AVOID TRAFFIC JAMS

Each FTP site can only let a certain number of people use the site at once. If you get an error message when you try to connect, the site may already have as many people connected as it can handle.

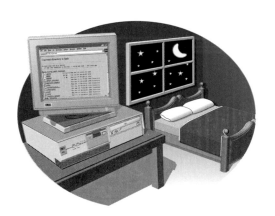

Connect at a Different Time

Try accessing FTP sites outside business hours, such as at night and on the weekend. Fewer people use the Internet at these times.

Use Mirror Sites

Some popular FTP sites have mirror sites. A mirror site stores exactly the same information as the original site, but is usually less busy. A mirror site may also be geographically closer to your computer, which can provide a faster and more reliable connection.

Mirror sites are updated on a regular basis to ensure that files available at the original site are also available at the mirror site.

CHAPTER 15:

COMPATIBILITY

Just because you can transfer a file to your computer does not mean you can use the file. Make sure you only get files that can work with your type of computer. Many FTP sites have separate directories for Macintosh and IBM-compatible computers.

HARDWARE AND SOFTWARE

You may need special hardware or software to use files you get from an FTP site. For example, you need a sound card and speakers to hear sound files.

VIRUSES

Files stored at FTP sites are not regulated and may contain viruses. A virus is a destructive computer program that can disrupt the normal operation of a computer.

Make sure you back up the files on your computer frequently and check for viruses before you use any file copied from an FTP site. Anti-virus programs are available at most major FTP sites.

COMPRESSED FILES

Many large files stored at FTP sites are compressed, or squeezed, to make them smaller.

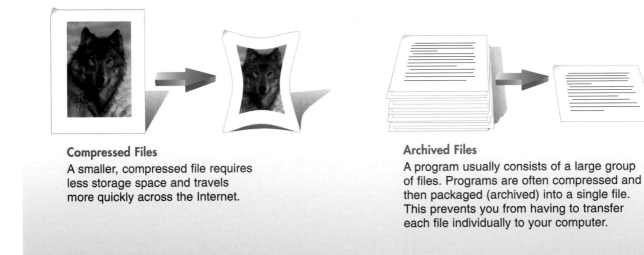

Compressed Files

A smaller, compressed file requires less storage space and travels more quickly across the Internet.

Archived Files

A program usually consists of a large group of files. Programs are often compressed and then packaged (archived) into a single file. This prevents you from having to transfer each file individually to your computer.

Compressed or archived files usually have one of the following extensions:

.arc .arj .gz .hqx .sit .tar .z .zip

Decompressed Files

Before you can use a compressed or archived file on your computer, you usually have to expand or unpack the file using a decompression program.

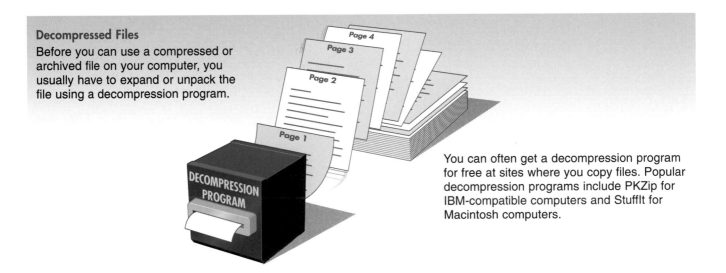

You can often get a decompression program for free at sites where you copy files. Popular decompression programs include PKZip for IBM-compatible computers and StuffIt for Macintosh computers.

SEARCH FOR FTP FILES

There are sites that let you search
for files available at FTP sites around
the world. This helps you find files of
interest to you.

ARCHIE

Archie lets you search for specific files you have
heard or read about. To use Archie, you need to
know part of the name of the file you want to find.

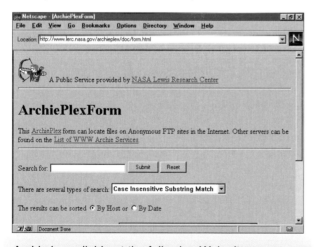

Archie is available at the following Web sites:

NASA
http://www.lerc.nasa.gov/archieplex

Rutgers University
http://www-ns.rutgers.edu/htbin/archie

SHAREWARE.COM

Shareware.com lets you search for specific
files or browse through files stored at FTP
sites around the world.

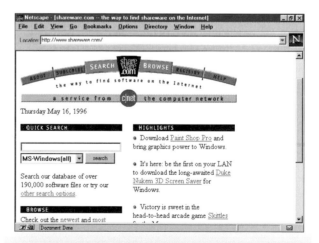

You can access shareware.com
at the following Web site:

http://www.shareware.com

INDEX

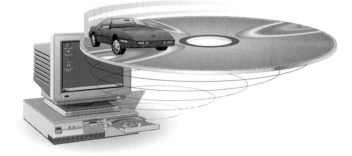

INDEX

ORGANIZATION

com	commercial
edu	education
gov	government
mil	military
net	network
org	organization (often non-profit)

INDEX

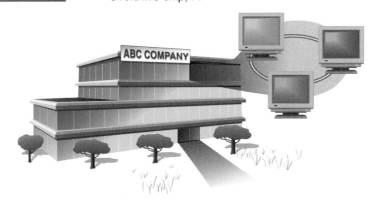

INDEX

P

packet, 182
parallel port, 14
passive matrix screen, 115
password
    Internet, 185
    network, 174
PC, 8
PC Card, 120
PCMCIA Card and slot, 120
peer-to-peer network, 170
Pentium CPU, 76
Pentium Pro CPU, 76
peripheral, 4
peripheral component interconnect (PCI) bus, 81
personal computer (PC), 8
platform, 153
Plug and Play, 81, 161
plug-in, 200
pointing device, 27
pointing stick, portable computer, 116
point-to-point protocol (PPP), 187
port, 14-15
port replicator, 121
portable, 12. *See also* portable computer
portable computer
    battery, 113
    CPU, 119
    keyboard, 117
    memory, 119
    modem, 117
    overview, 112
    pointing device, 116
    screen, 114-115
    sound card, 117
    speaker, 117
    storage device, 118
Postscript, 40
power supply, 10, 13
pretty good privacy (PGP), 237

print
    buffer, 45
    feature in programs, 42-43
    spooler, 45
printer, 9, 32-45
    Bubble Jet, 36
    considerations when choosing, 32
    dot-matrix, 34-35
    dye sublimation, 41
    ink jet, 36-37
    laser, 38-40
    multifunction laser, 39
    overview, 32
    resolution, 33
    solid ink, 41
    speed, 33
    thermal-wax, 41
printer control language (PCL), 40
privacy enhanced mail (PEM), 237
private FTP site, 270
program. *See also* software
    anti-virus, 92
    at FTP sites, 273
    e-mail, 229
    for connecting to Internet, 184
    freeware, 273
    icon, 157
    newsreader, 253
    on Internet, 180
    overview, 124
    public domain, 273
    shareware, 273
public domain program, 273

INDEX

tower case, 12
trackball, 27
    portable computer, 116
traffic
    at FTP sites, 274
    on network, 169
    on Web, 192
Travan drive, 109
TrueType font, 44

U

uniform resource locator (URL), 193
uninterruptible power supply (UPS), 13
universal serial bus (USB), 15
unshielded twisted pair (UTP) cable, 169
Usenet, 252
user name, 230
    Internet, 185
    network, 174
uudecode, 260
uuencode, 260

V

version, software, 125
video
    at FTP sites, 272
    on Web, 203
video card
    memory, 51
    overview, 46

video graphics array (VGA) monitor, 53
video local bus (VL-Bus), 81
video random access memory (VRAM), 51
videoconferencing, 168
virtual memory, 73
virtual reality modeling language (VRML), 203
virus, 92, 275

W

wavetable synthesis, 65
Web
    browser, 194-195
    chat on, 265
    multimedia on, 200-203
    overview, 192-193
    page, 192. *See also* Web site
        create and publish, 208-213
        form, 198
        frame, 198
        table, 198
    search, 204-207
    security, 197
    server, 212
    shopping on, 196
    site, 192. *See also* Web page
        examples, 216-225
    3-D worlds, 203
wide area network (WAN), 166
window RAM (WRAM), 51
Windows for Workgroups 3.11 (WfWG), 159
Windows 95, 160-163
Windows NT, 163
Windows 3.1, 156-159
word processor, 126-131
World Wide Web. *See* Web
wrist rest, 19
W3. *See* Web
WWW. *See* Web
WYSIWYG, 42

Z

zero insertion force (ZIF) socket, 77

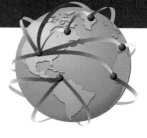
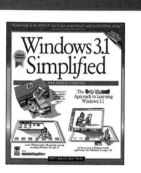

**DOS For Dummies,®
2nd Edition**
by Dan Gookin

ISBN: 1-878058-75-4
$16.95 USA/$22.95 Canada

**The Internet
For Dummies™**
*by John Levine &
Carol Baroudi*

ISBN: 1-56884-024-1
$19.95 USA/$26.95 Canada

**Macs For Dummies™
2nd Edition**
by David Pogue

ISBN: 1-56884-051-9
$19.95 USA/$26.95 Canada

ORDER FORM

IDG BOOKS

TRADE & INDIVIDUAL ORDERS

Phone: **(800) 762-2974**
or **(317) 895-5200**
(8 a.m.–6 p.m., CST, weekdays)
FAX : **(317) 895-5298**

EDUCATIONAL ORDERS & DISCOUNTS

Phone: **(800) 434-2086**
(8:30 a.m.–5:00 p.m., CST, weekdays)
FAX : **(817) 251-8174**

CORPORATE ORDERS FOR 3-D VISUAL™ SERIES

Phone: **(800) 469-6616**
(8 a.m.–5 p.m., EST, weekdays)
FAX : **(905) 890-9434**

Qty	ISBN	Title	Price	Total

Shipping & Handling Charges

	Description	First book	Each add'l. book	Total
Domestic	Normal	$4.50	$1.50	$
	Two Day Air	$8.50	$2.50	$
	Overnight	$18.00	$3.00	$
International	Surface	$8.00	$8.00	$
	Airmail	$16.00	$16.00	$
	DHL Air	$17.00	$17.00	$

Subtotal _____

CA residents add
applicable sales tax _____

IN, MA and MD
residents add
5% sales tax _____

IL residents add
6.25% sales tax _____

RI residents add
7% sales tax _____

TX residents add
8.25% sales tax _____

Shipping _____

Total _____

Ship to:

Name _____

Address _____

Company _____

City/State/Zip _____

Daytime Phone _____

Payment: □ Check to IDG Books (US Funds Only)

□ Visa   □ Mastercard   □ American Express

Card # _____ Exp. _____ Signature _____

maranGraphics™

IDG BOOKS WORLDWIDE REGISTRATION CARD

RETURN THIS REGISTRATION CARD FOR FREE CATALOG

Title of this book: Teach Yourself Computers and the Internet VISUALLY™

My overall rating of this book: ❑ Very good [1] ❑ Good [2] ❑ Satisfactory [3] ❑ Fair [4] ❑ Poor [5]

How I first heard about this book:

❑ Found in bookstore; name: [6] _____   ❑ Book review: [7]

❑ Advertisement: [8]   ❑ Catalog: [9]

❑ Word of mouth; heard about book from friend, co-worker, etc.: [10]   ❑ Other: [11]

What I liked most about this book:

_____

_____

What I would change, add, delete, etc., in future editions of this book:

_____

_____

Other comments:

_____

_____

Number of computer books I purchase in a year: ❑ 1 [12] ❑ 2-5 [13] ❑ 6-10 [14] ❑ More than 10 [15]

I would characterize my computer skills as: ❑ Beginner [16] ❑ Intermediate [17] ❑ Advanced [18] ❑ Professional [19]

I use ❑ DOS [20] ❑ Windows [21] ❑ OS/2 [22] ❑ Unix [23] ❑ Macintosh [24] ❑ Other: [25] _____
(please specify)

I would be interested in new books on the following subjects:
(please check all that apply, and use the spaces provided to identify specific software)

❑ Word processing: [26]   ❑ Spreadsheets: [27]

❑ Data bases: [28]   ❑ Desktop publishing: [29]

❑ File Utilities: [30]   ❑ Money management: [31]

❑ Networking: [32]   ❑ Programming languages: [33]

❑ Other: [34]

I use a PC at (please check all that apply): ❑ home [35] ❑ work [36] ❑ school [37] ❑ other: [38] _____

The disks I prefer to use are ❑ 5.25 [39] ❑ 3.5 [40] ❑ other: [41] _____

I have a CD ROM: ❑ yes [42] ❑ no [43]

I plan to buy or upgrade computer hardware this year: ❑ yes [44] ❑ no [45]

I plan to buy or upgrade computer software this year: ❑ yes [46] ❑ no [47]

Name: _____   Business title: [48] _____   Type of Business: [49] _____

Address (❑ home [50] ❑ work [51]/Company name: _____)

Street/Suite# _____

City [52]/State [53]/Zipcode [54]: _____   Country [55] _____

❑ **I liked this book!** You may quote me by name in future
IDG Books Worldwide promotional materials.

My daytime phone number is _____

IDG BOOKS®

THE WORLD OF
COMPUTER
KNOWLEDGE

❏ YES!

Please keep me informed about IDG's World of Computer Knowledge.
Send me the latest IDG Books catalog.

BUSINESS REPLY MAIL
FIRST CLASS MAIL   PERMIT NO. 2605   FOSTER CITY, CALIFORNIA

IDG Books Worldwide
919 E Hillsdale Blvd, STE 400
Foster City, CA 94404-9691

NO POSTAGE
NECESSARY
IF MAILED
IN THE
UNITED STATES